Easy Mandalas 2

Adult Coloring Book

Marg Ruttan

Featuring thirty easy mandalas to color, this adult coloring book will provide you with hours of coloring fun. Relax and enjoy these designs as you choose your color palate and bring them to life.

These mandalas have specifically been created to be easy to color and are for anyone who wants to relax and just enjoy their coloring activities without having to concentrate on intricate details. They are great for seniors and younger colorists who may need less detail in their mandalas.

Coloring has been proven to help us relax and relieve stress. It is my hope that this book can do that for you.

If you would like some free coloring pages and some good coloring tips, visit my website at www. coloringfunforadults.com

And to join my newsletter and receive five free coloring pages just go to www.coloringfunforadults. com/subscribe and sign up.

Happy Coloring,
Marg

Copyright
Copyright © 2015 By Marg Ruttan
All rights reserved.

Bibliographical Note:
Easy Mandalas 1 is a new work, first published by
Blue Jeans Publishing in 2016

International Standard Book Number
ISBN - 978-0-9734357-1-9

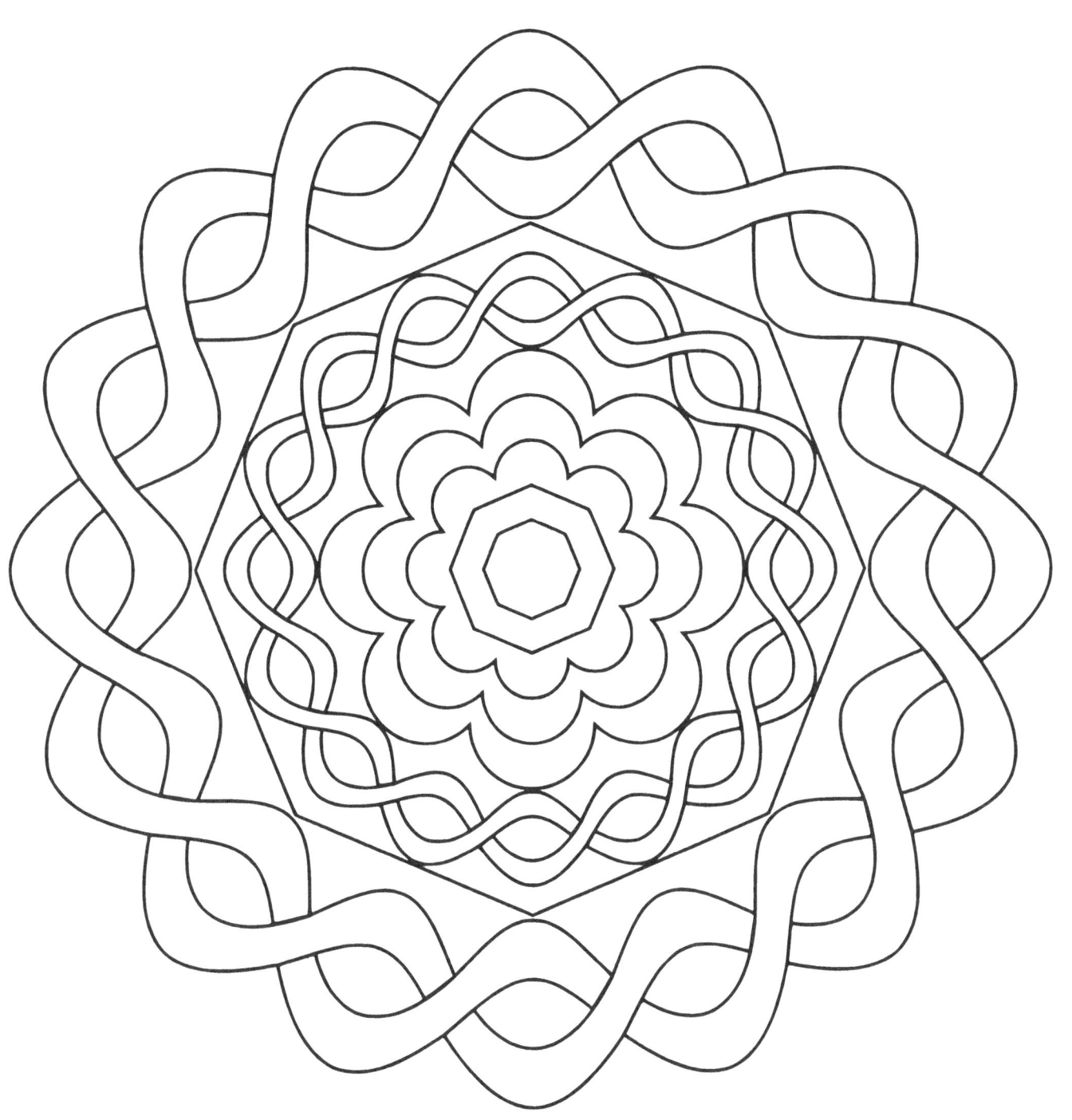

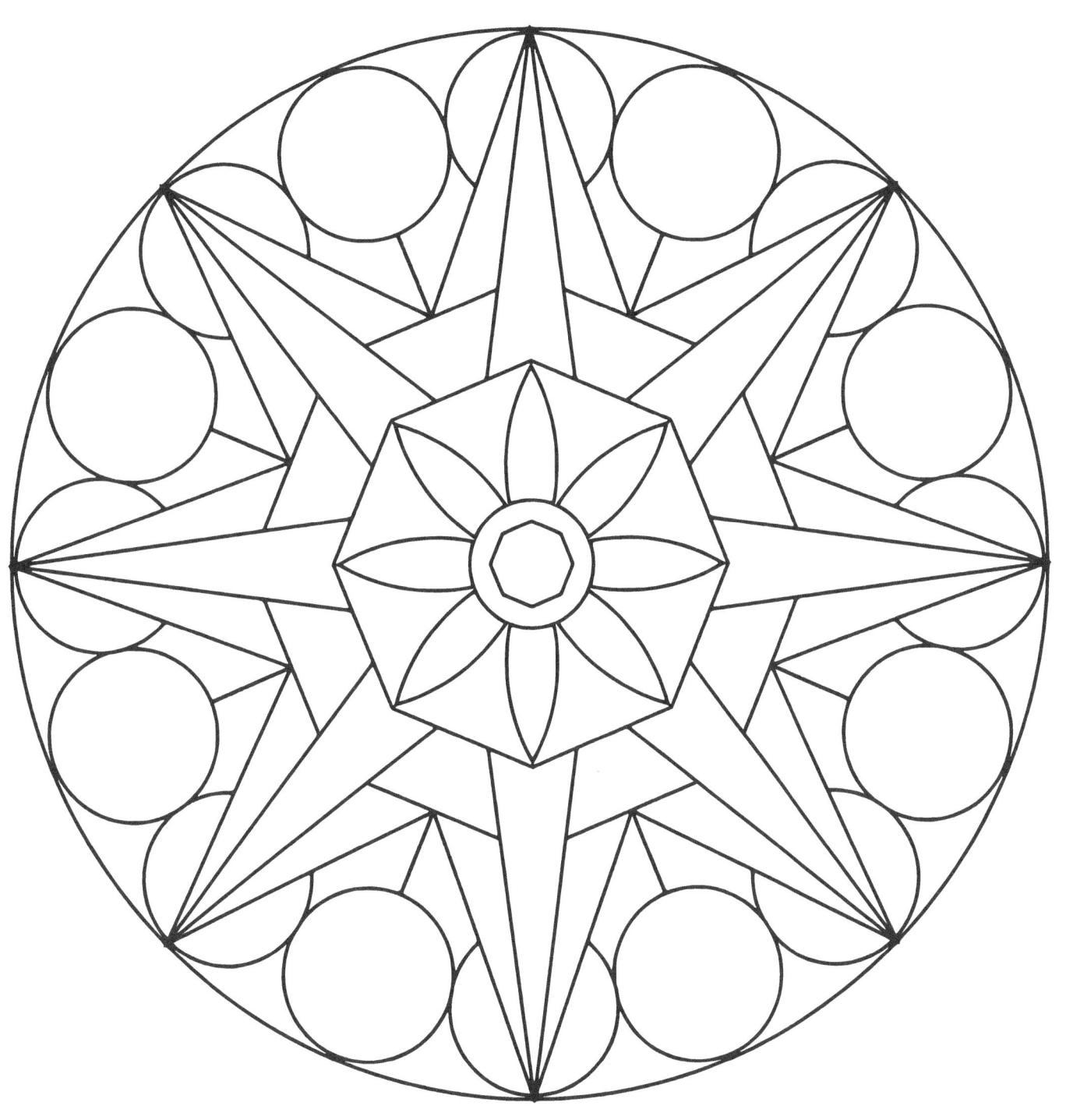

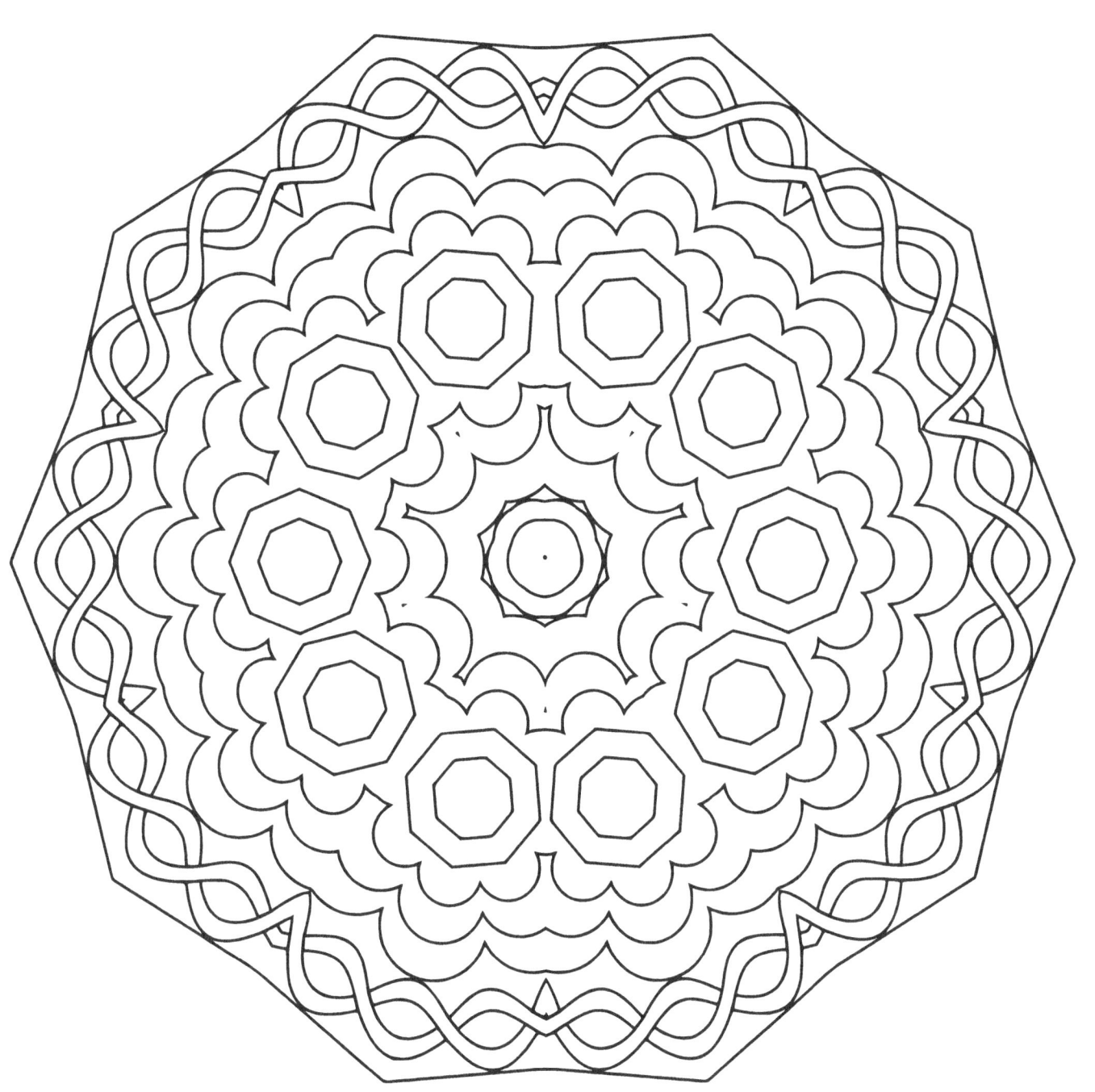

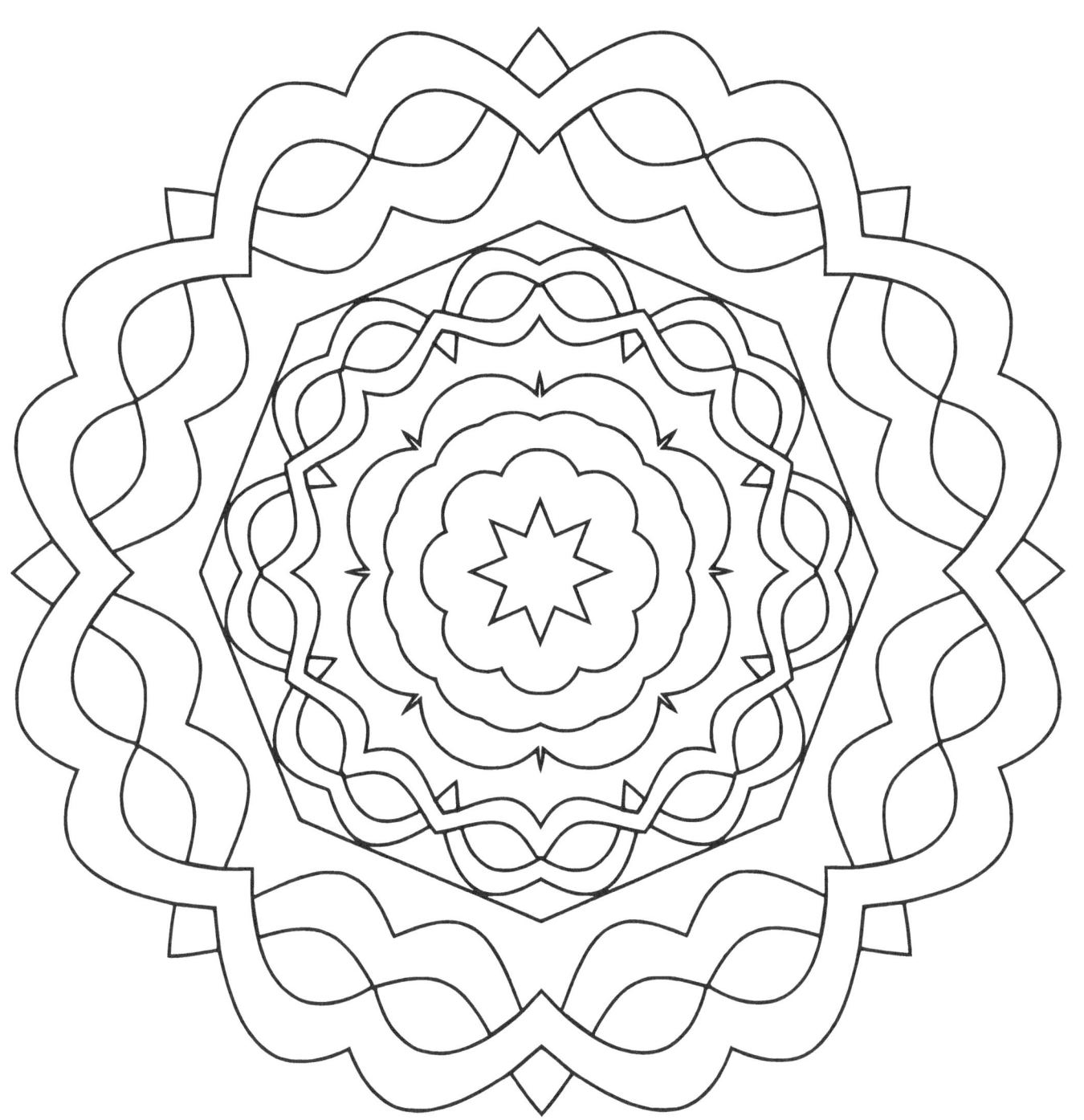

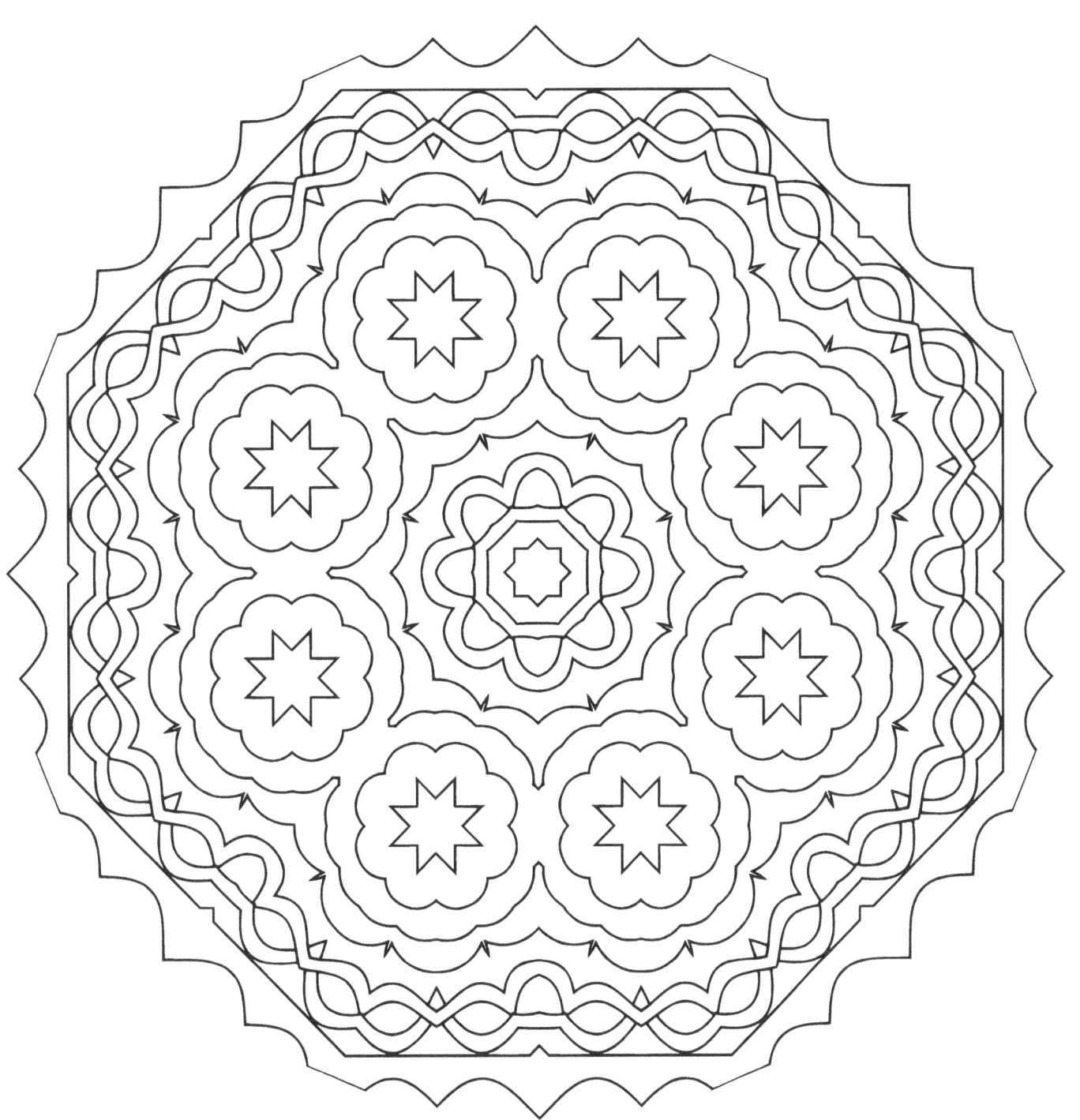

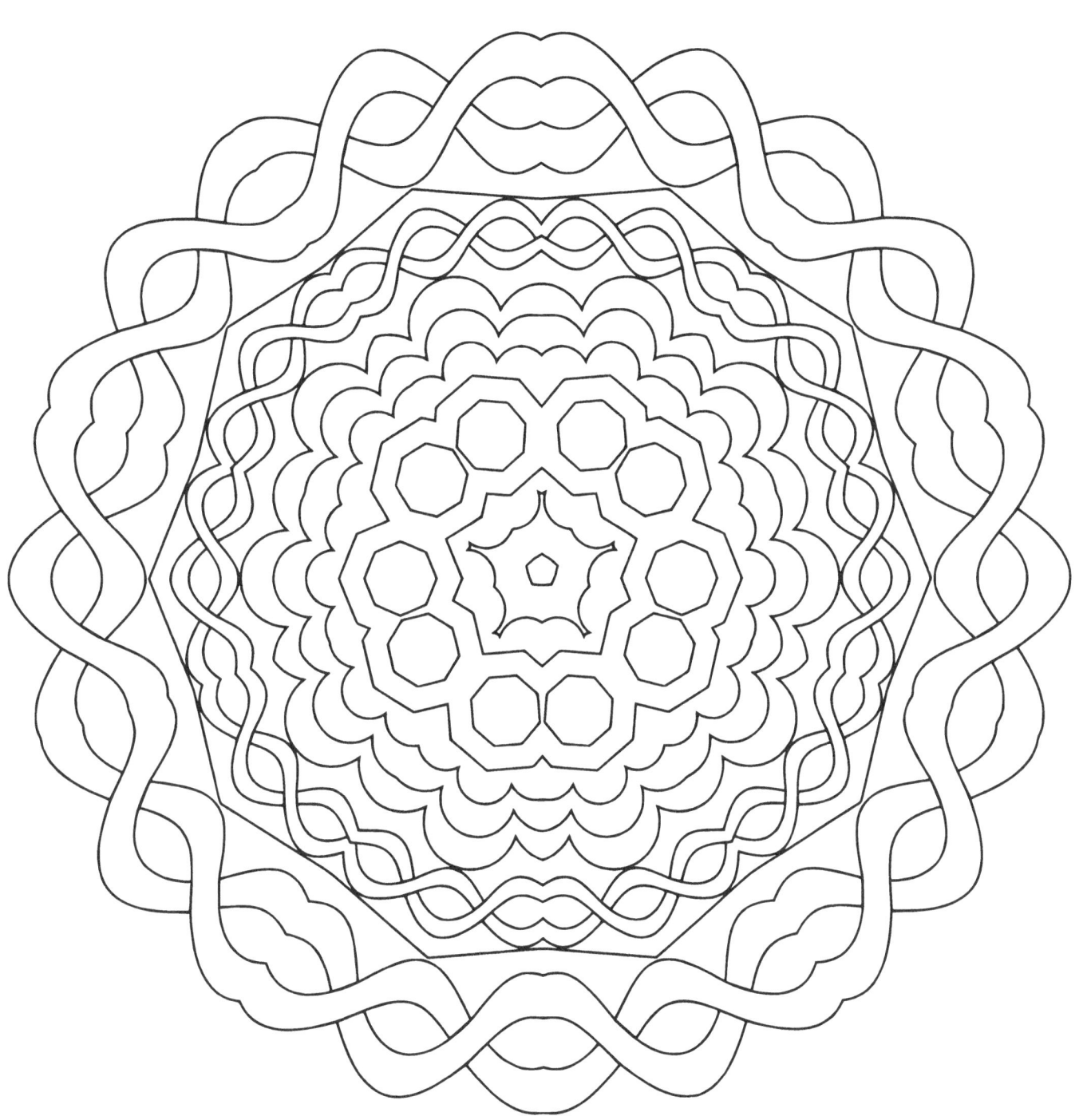

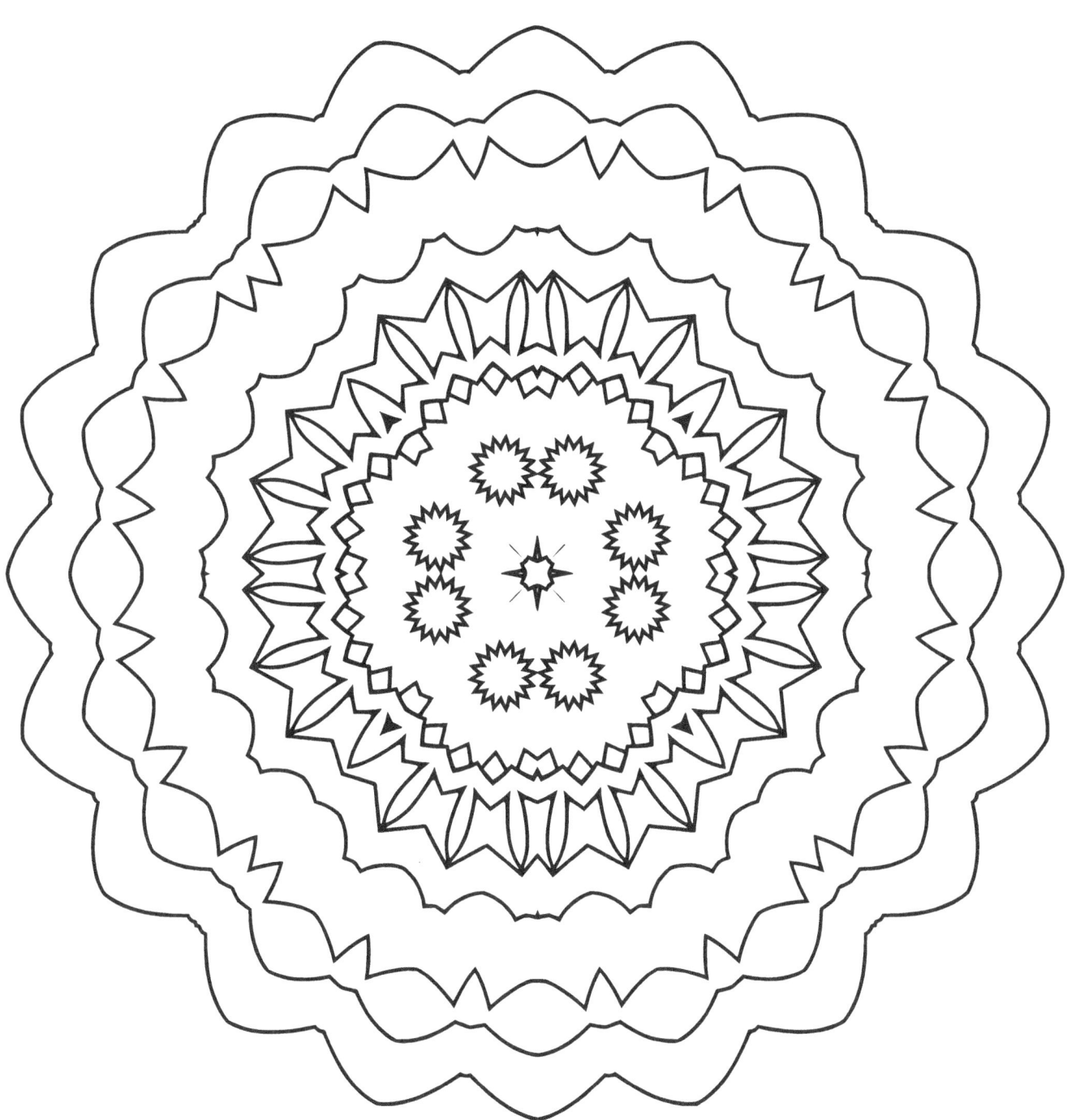

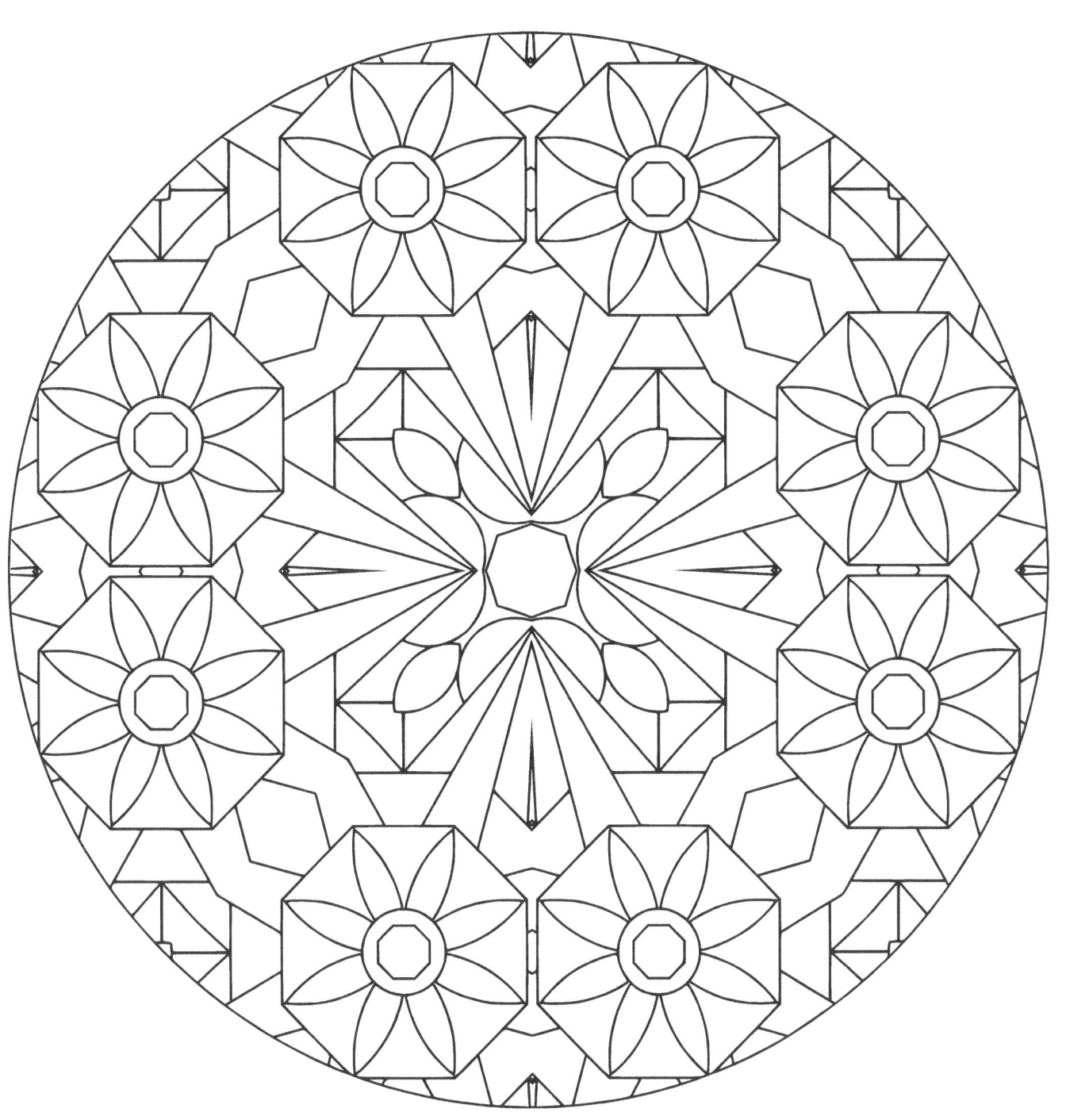

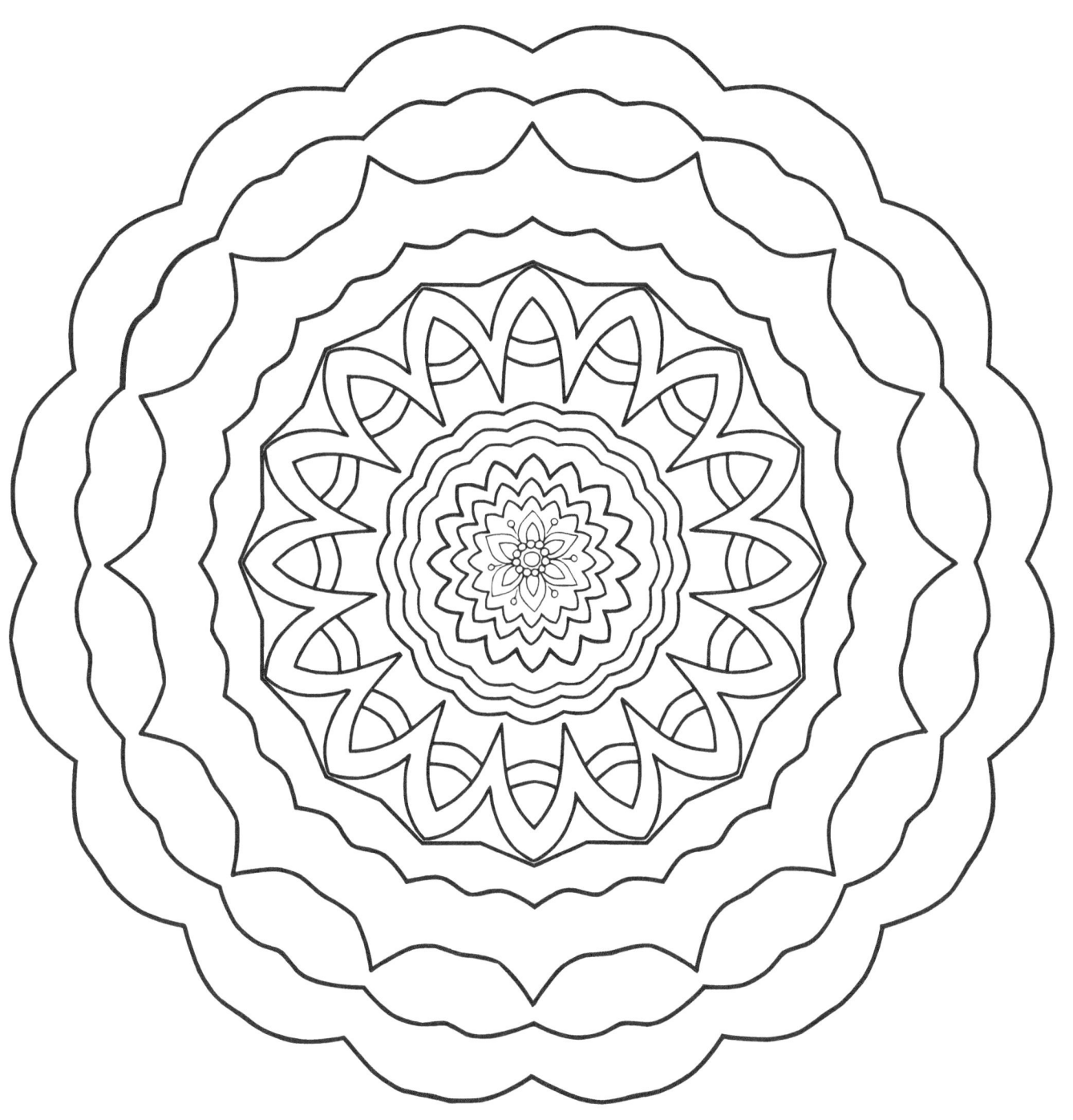

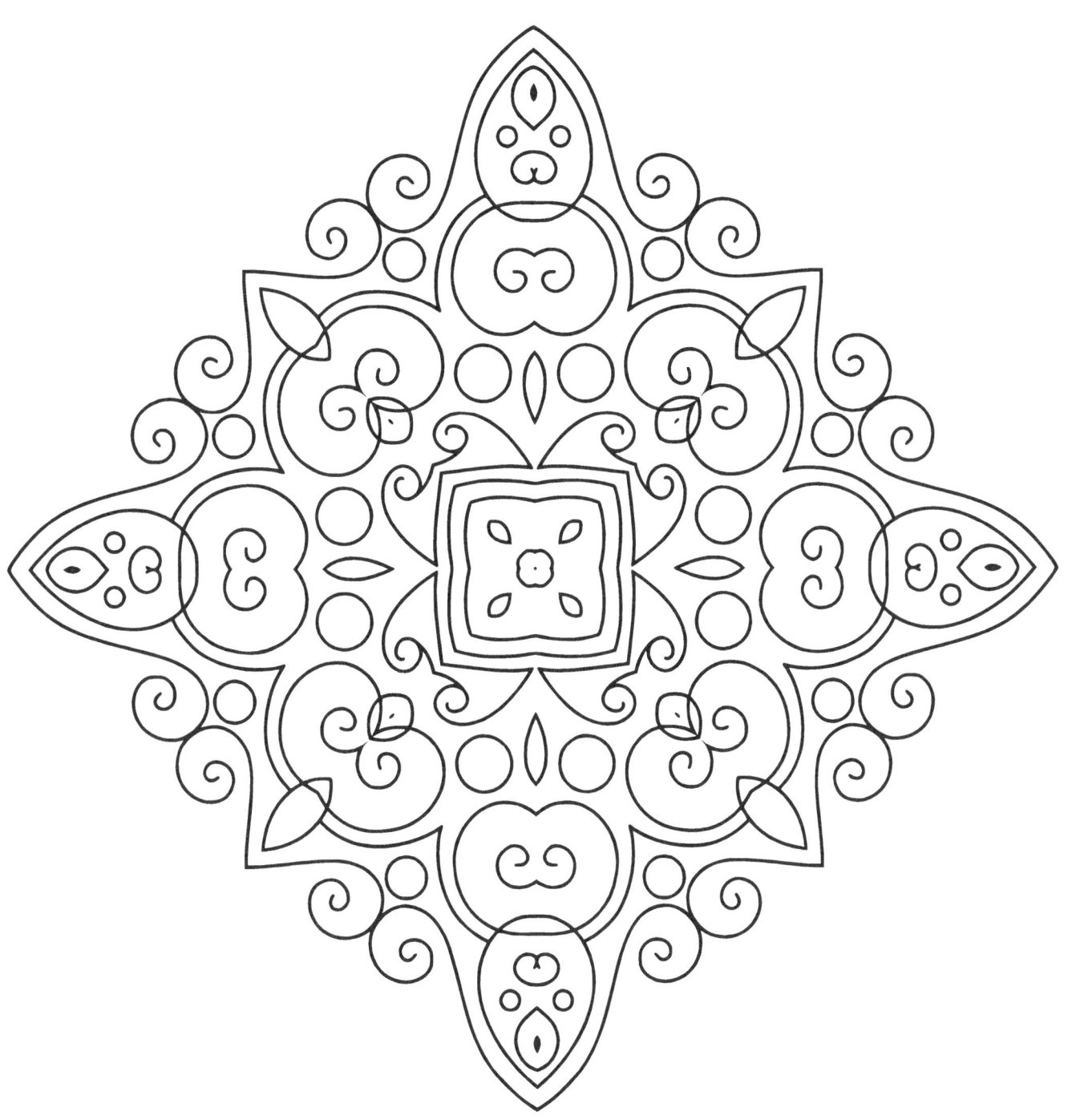

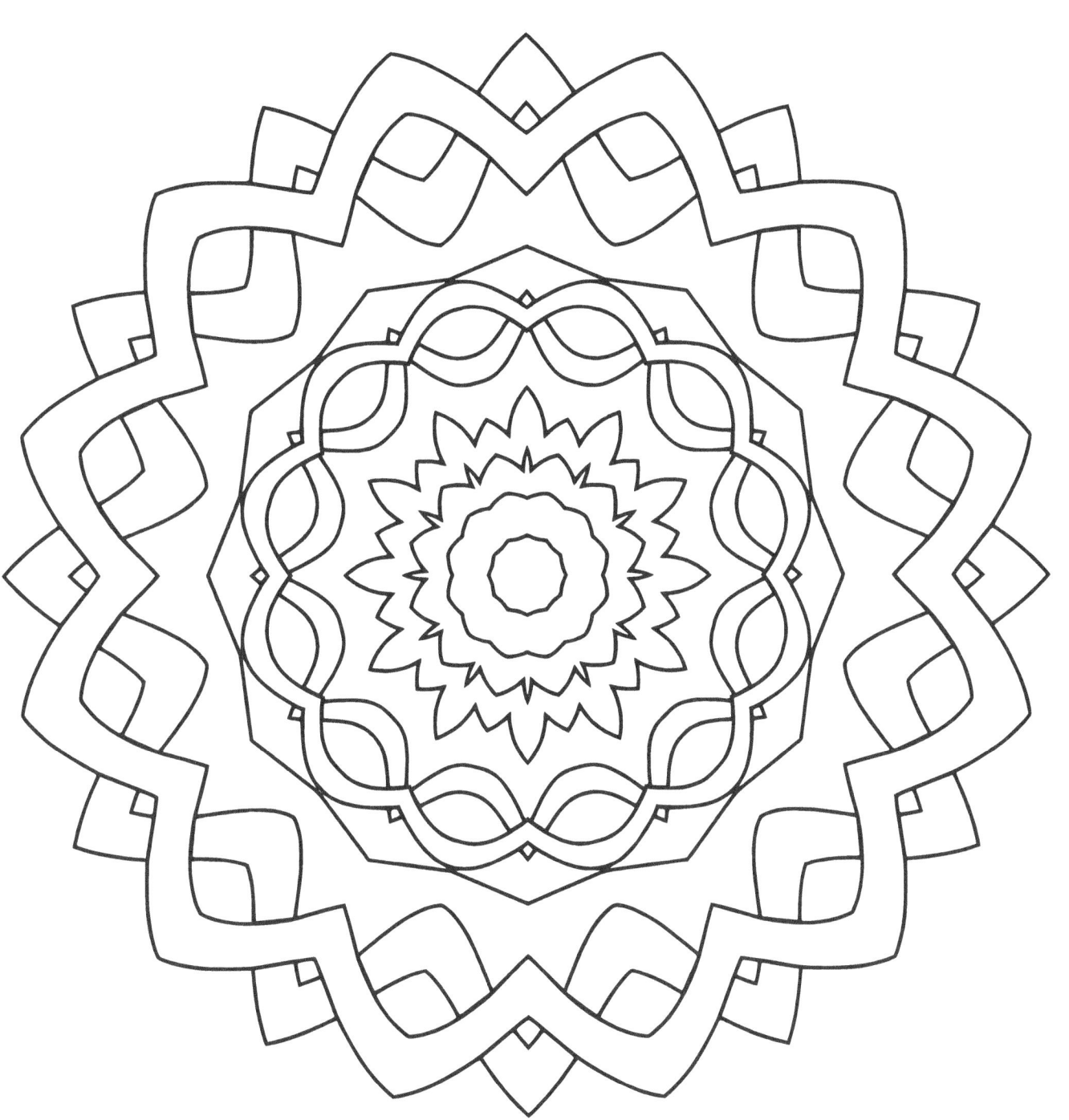

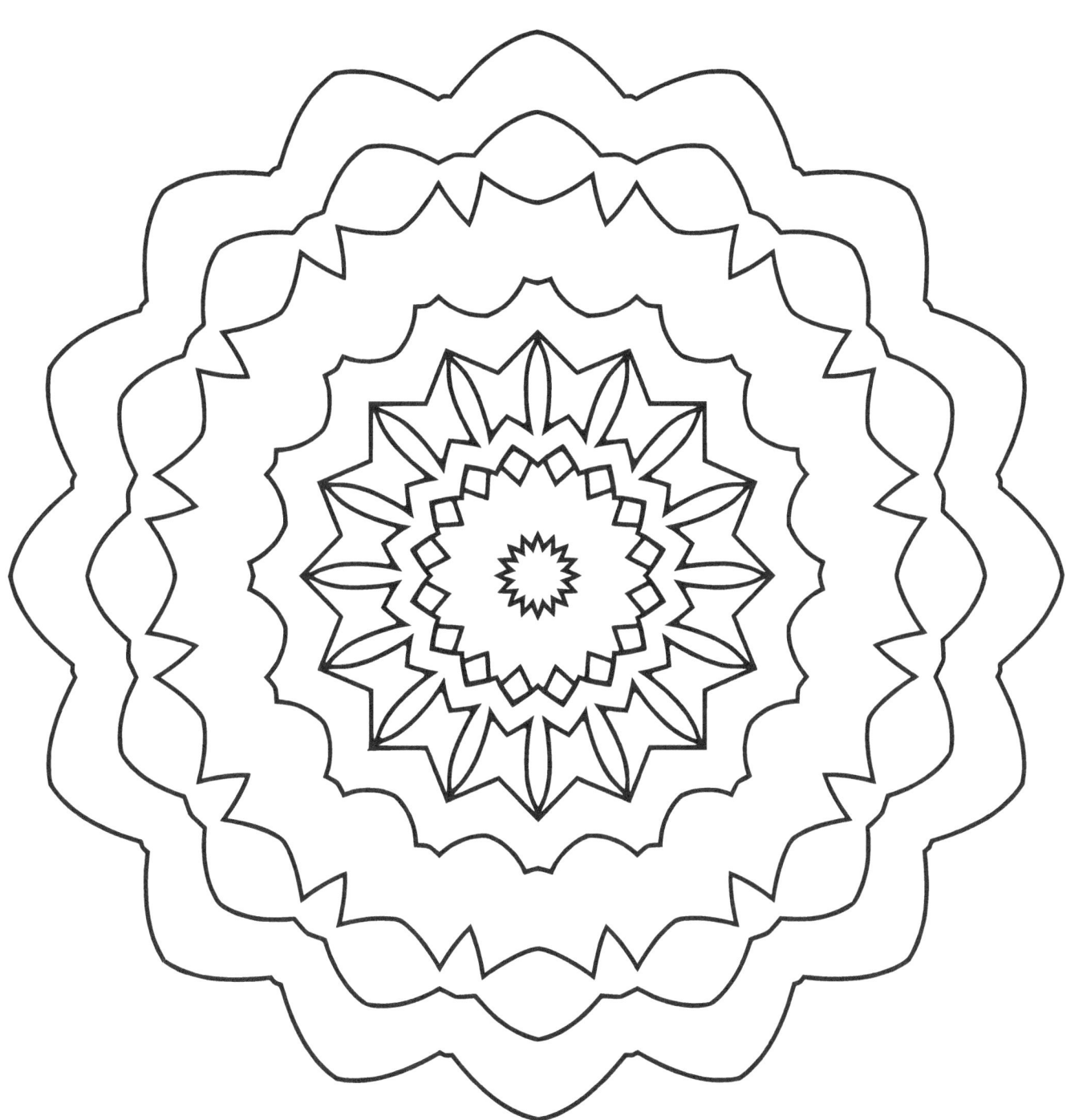

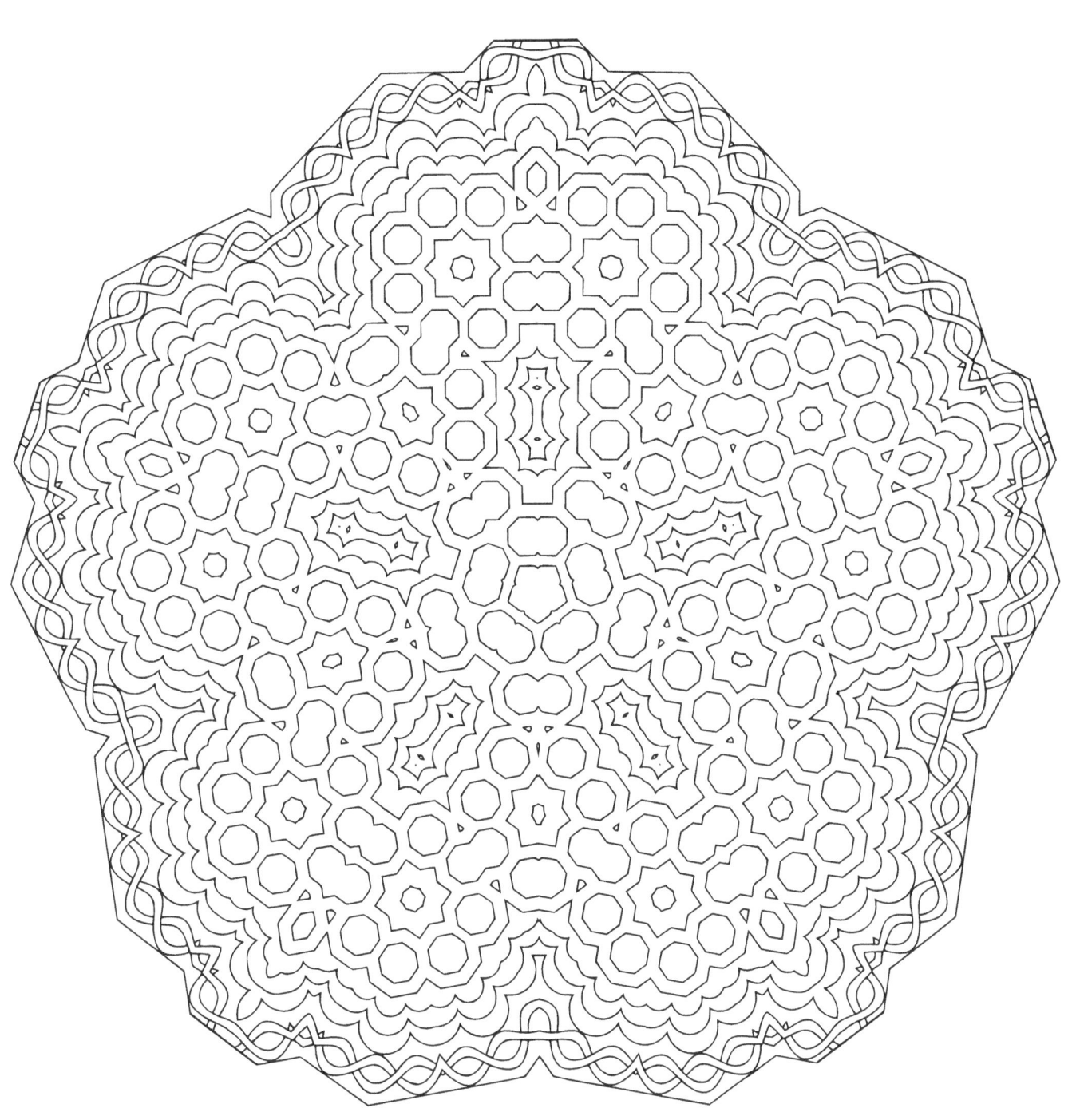

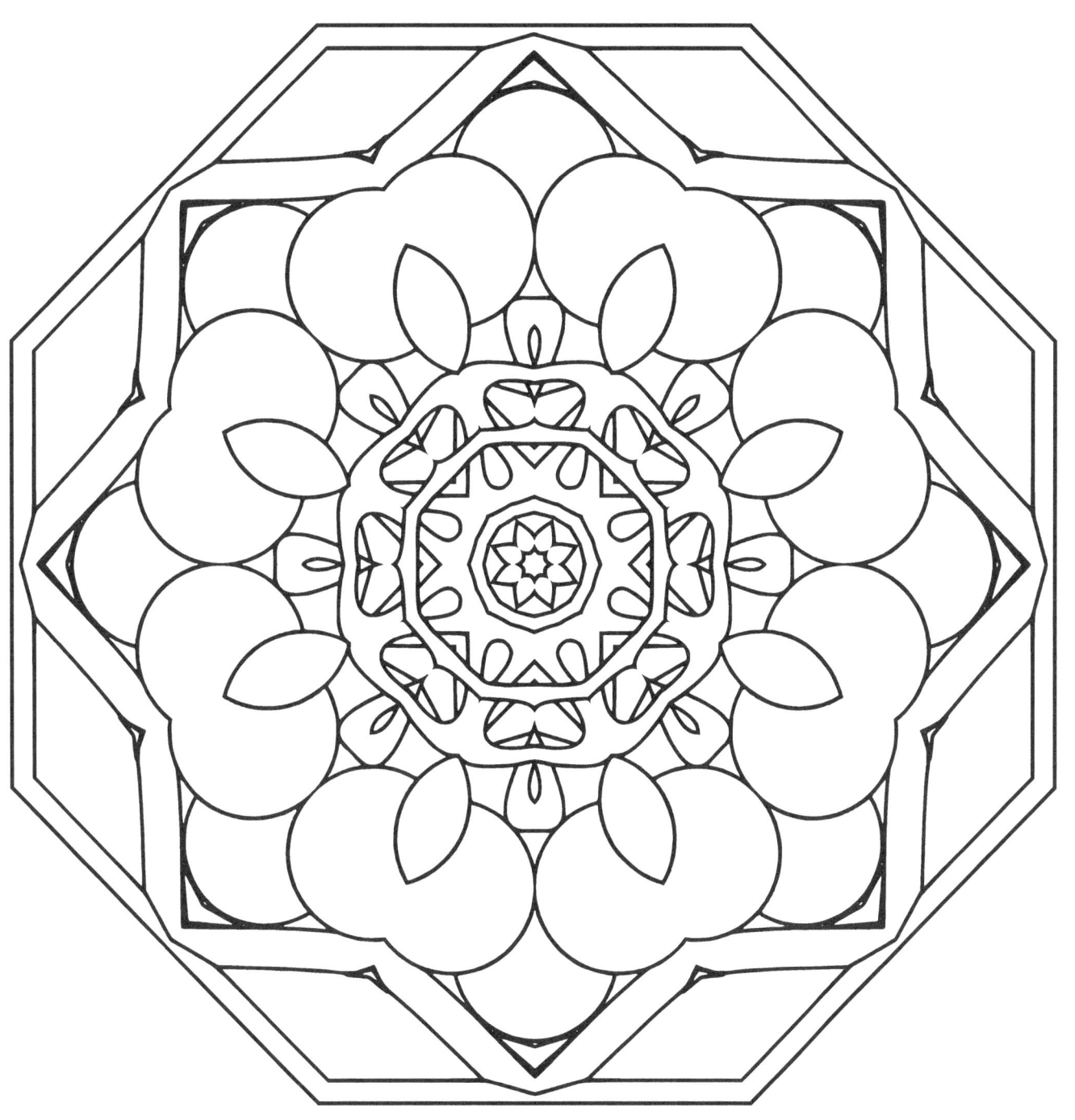

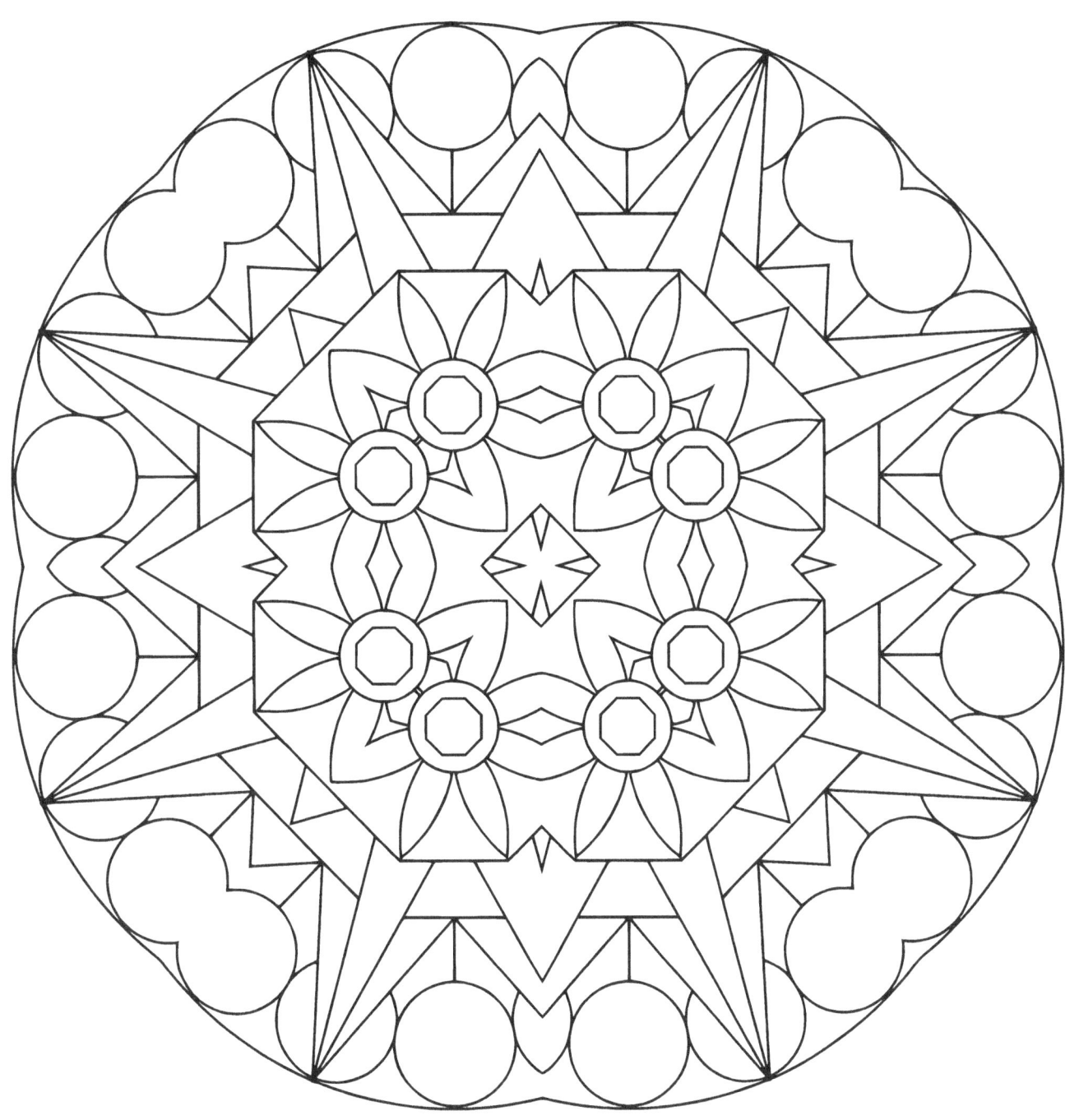

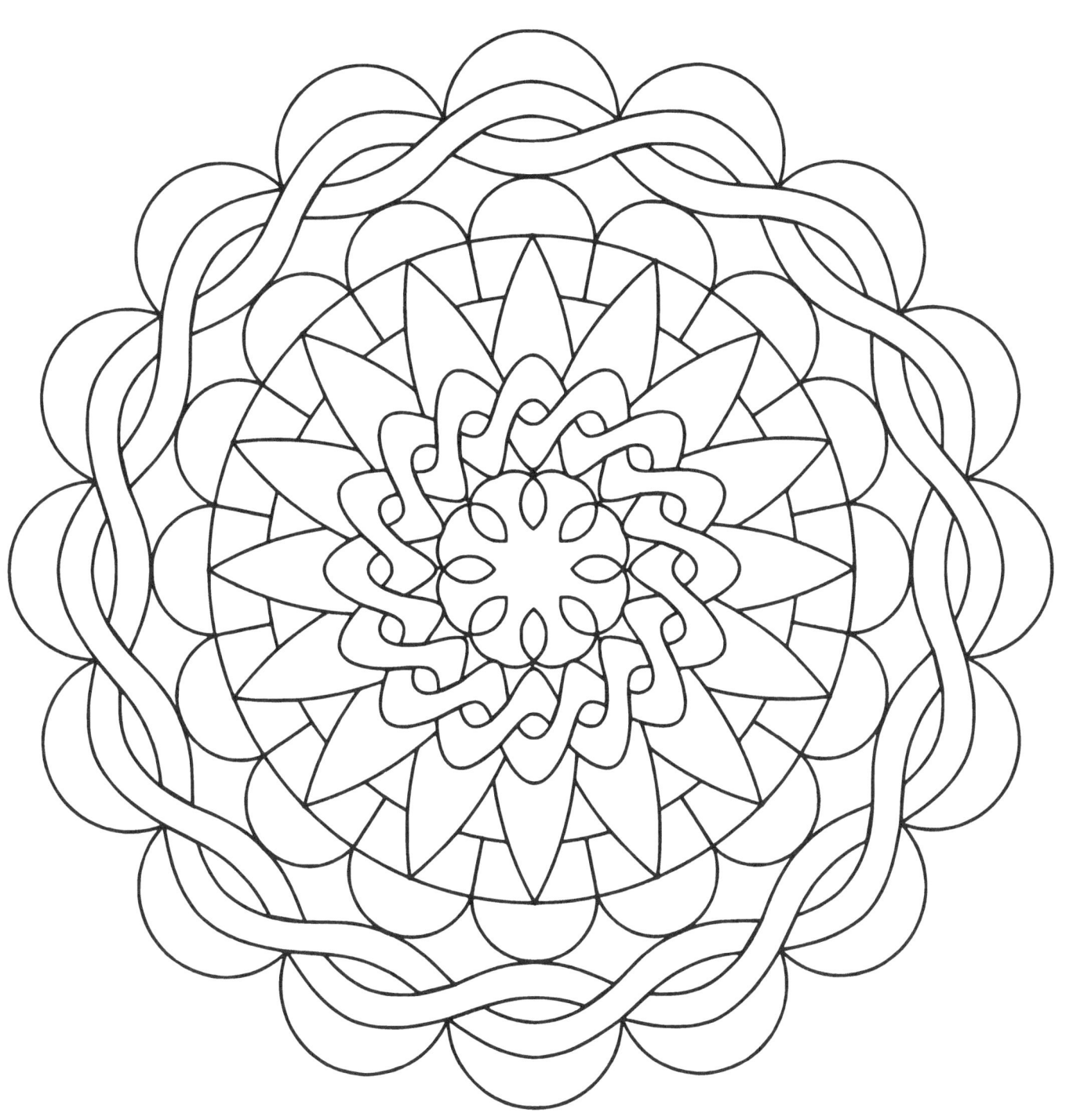

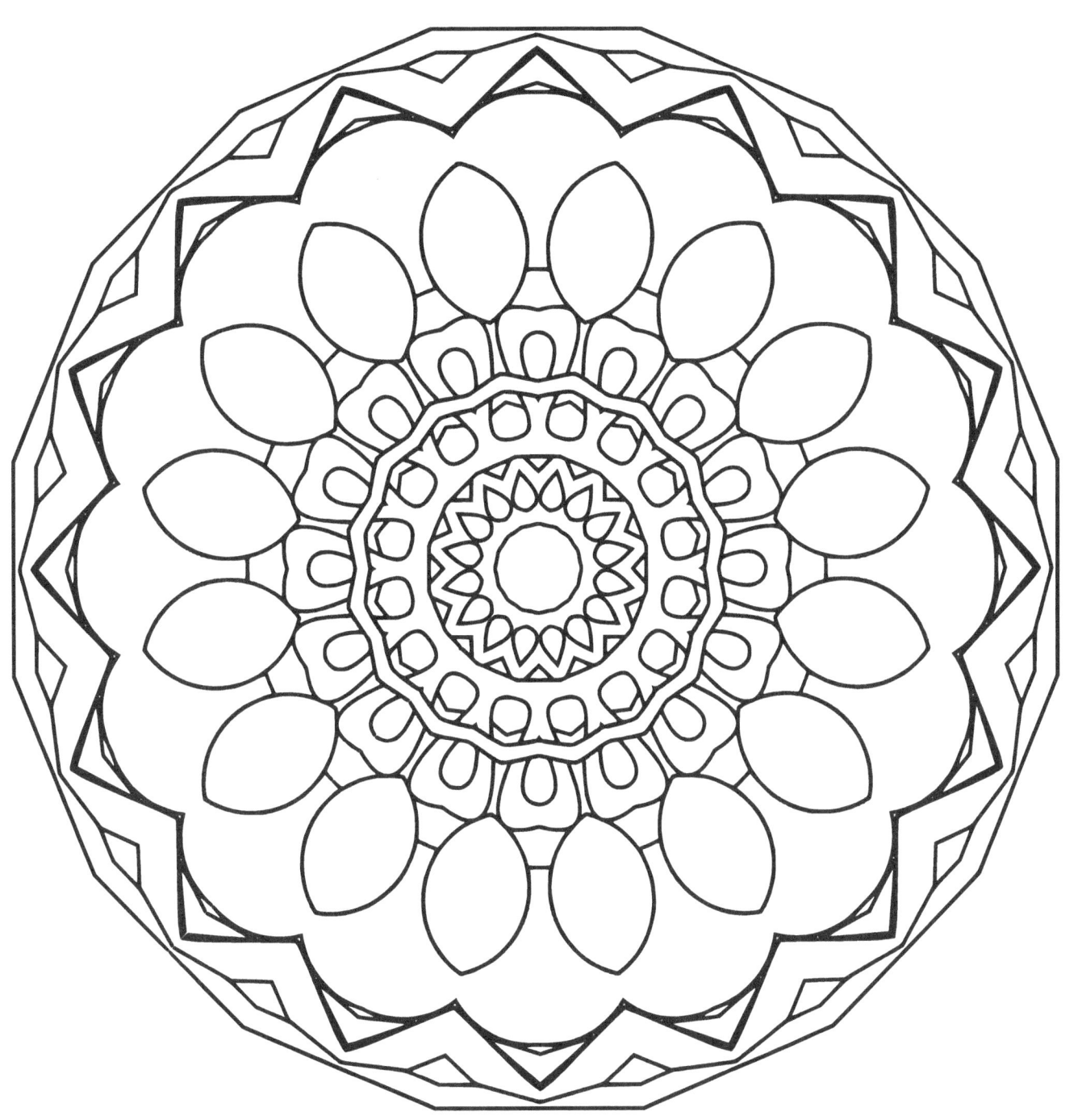

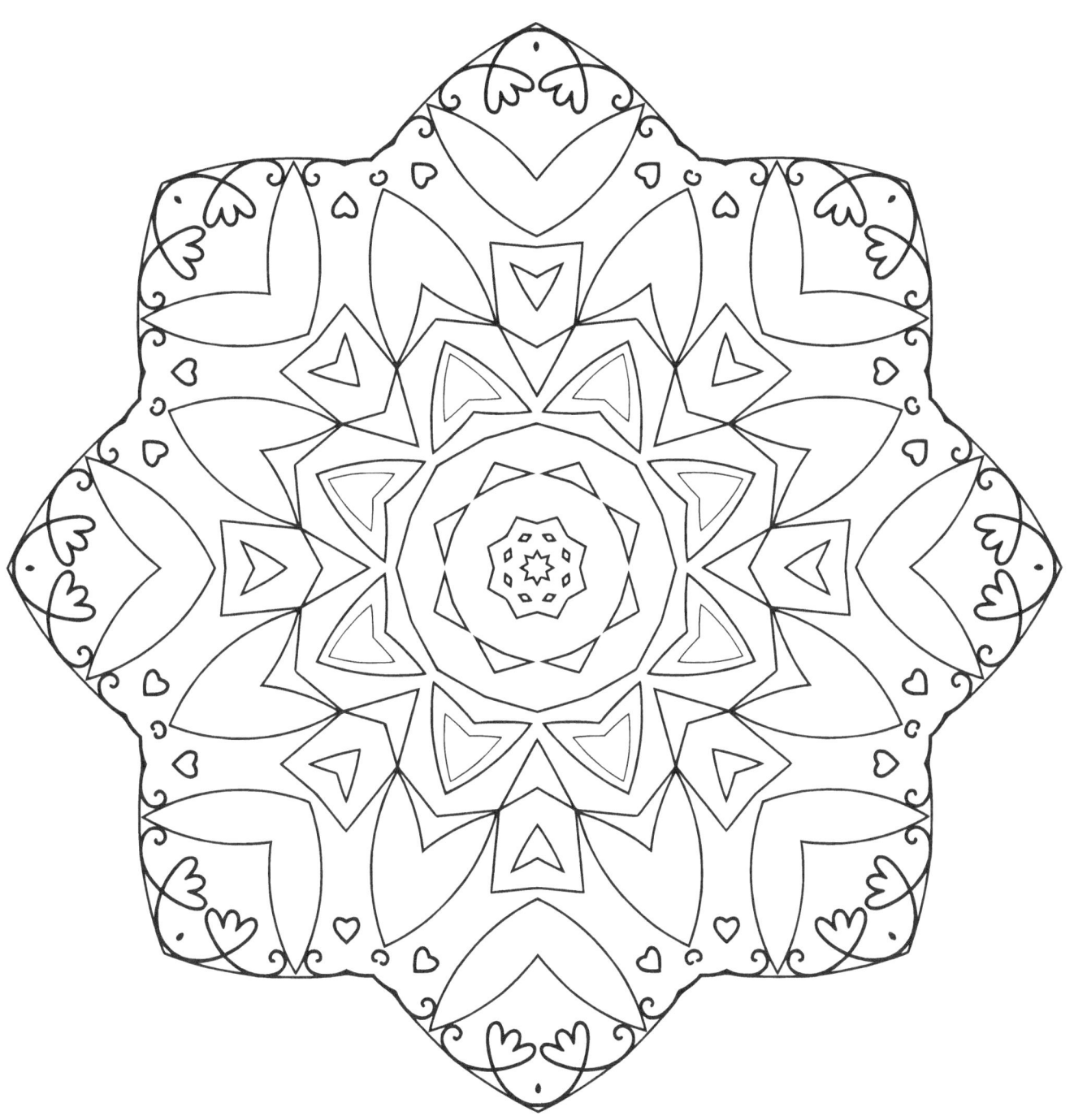

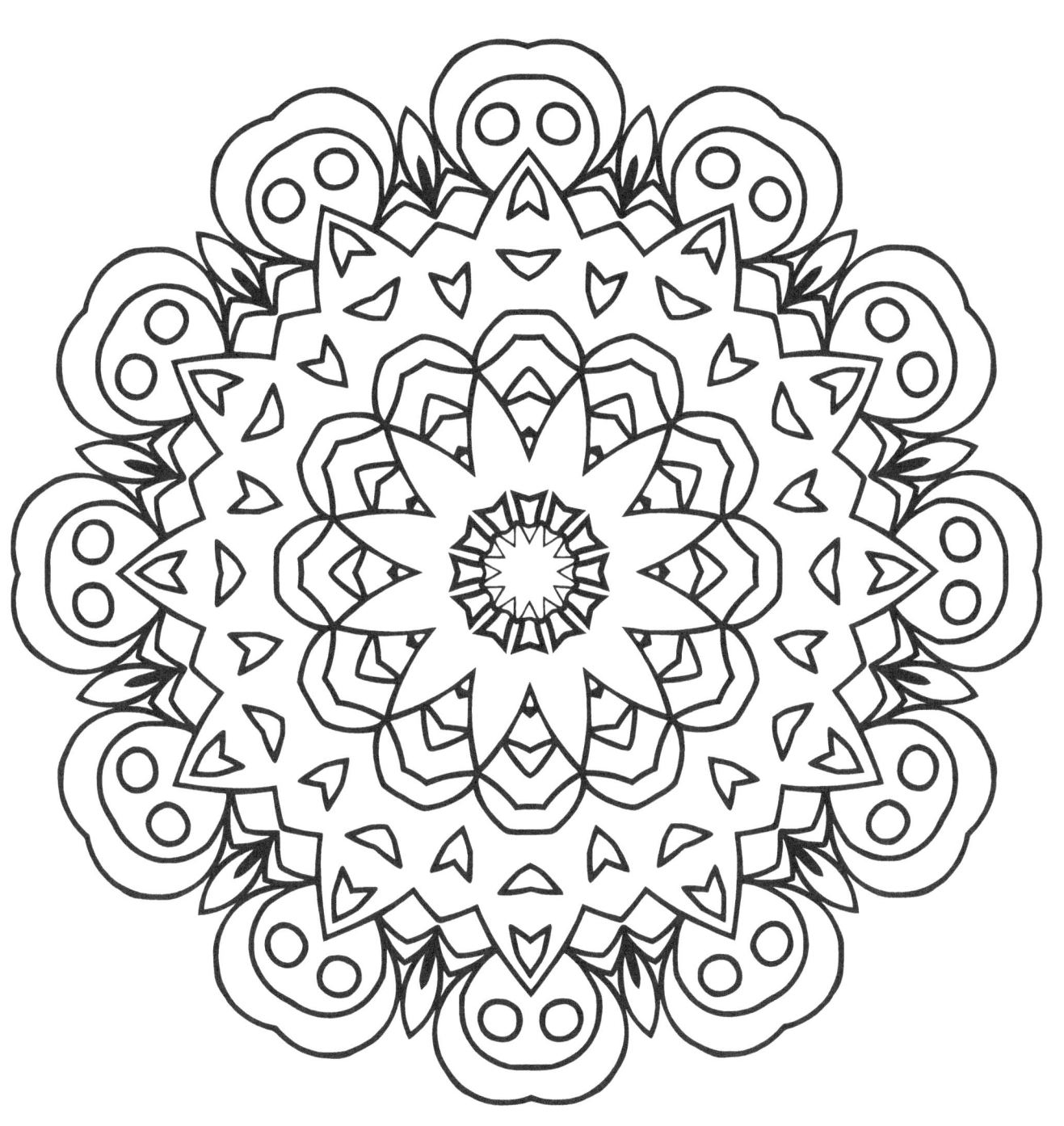

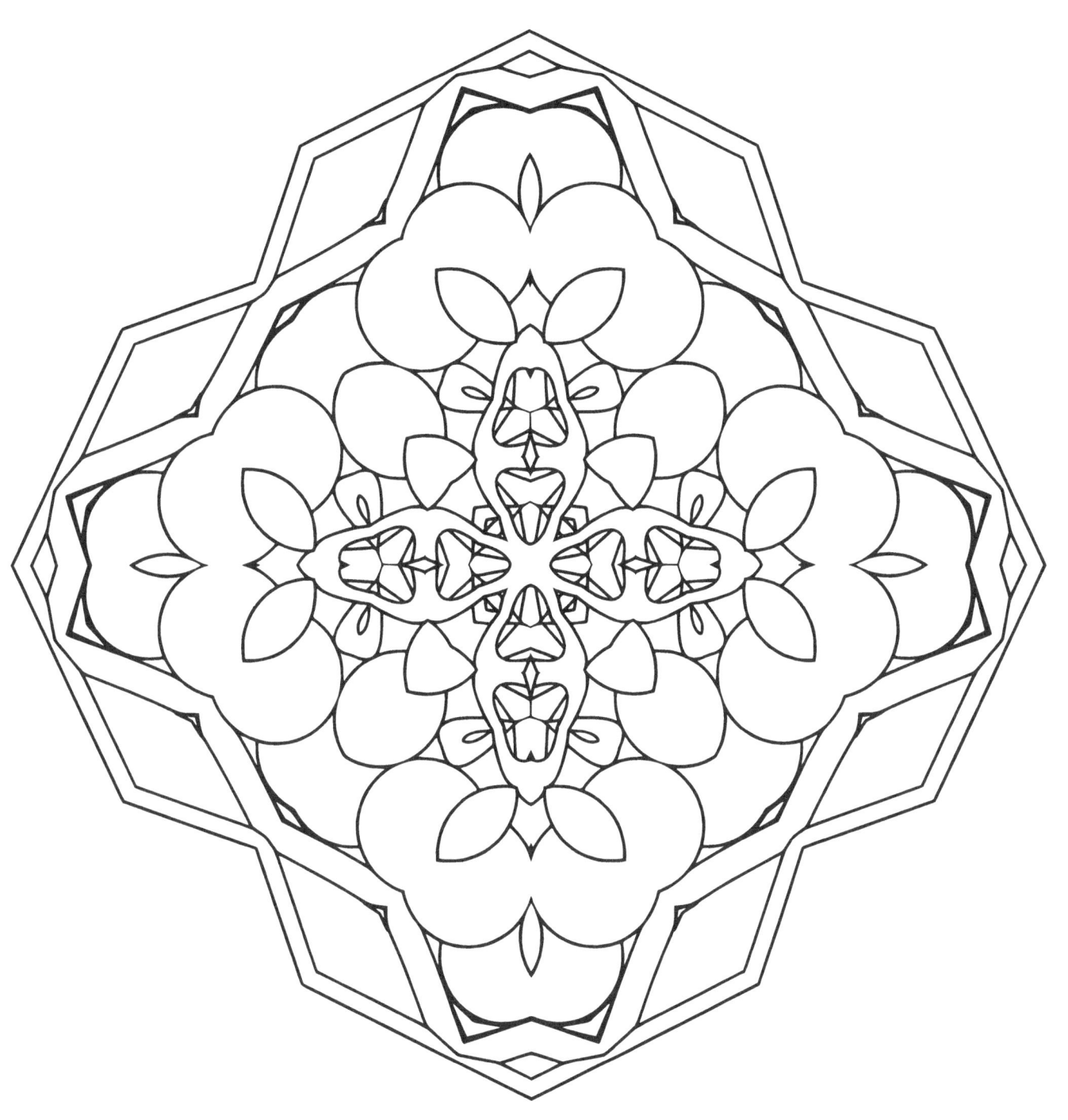

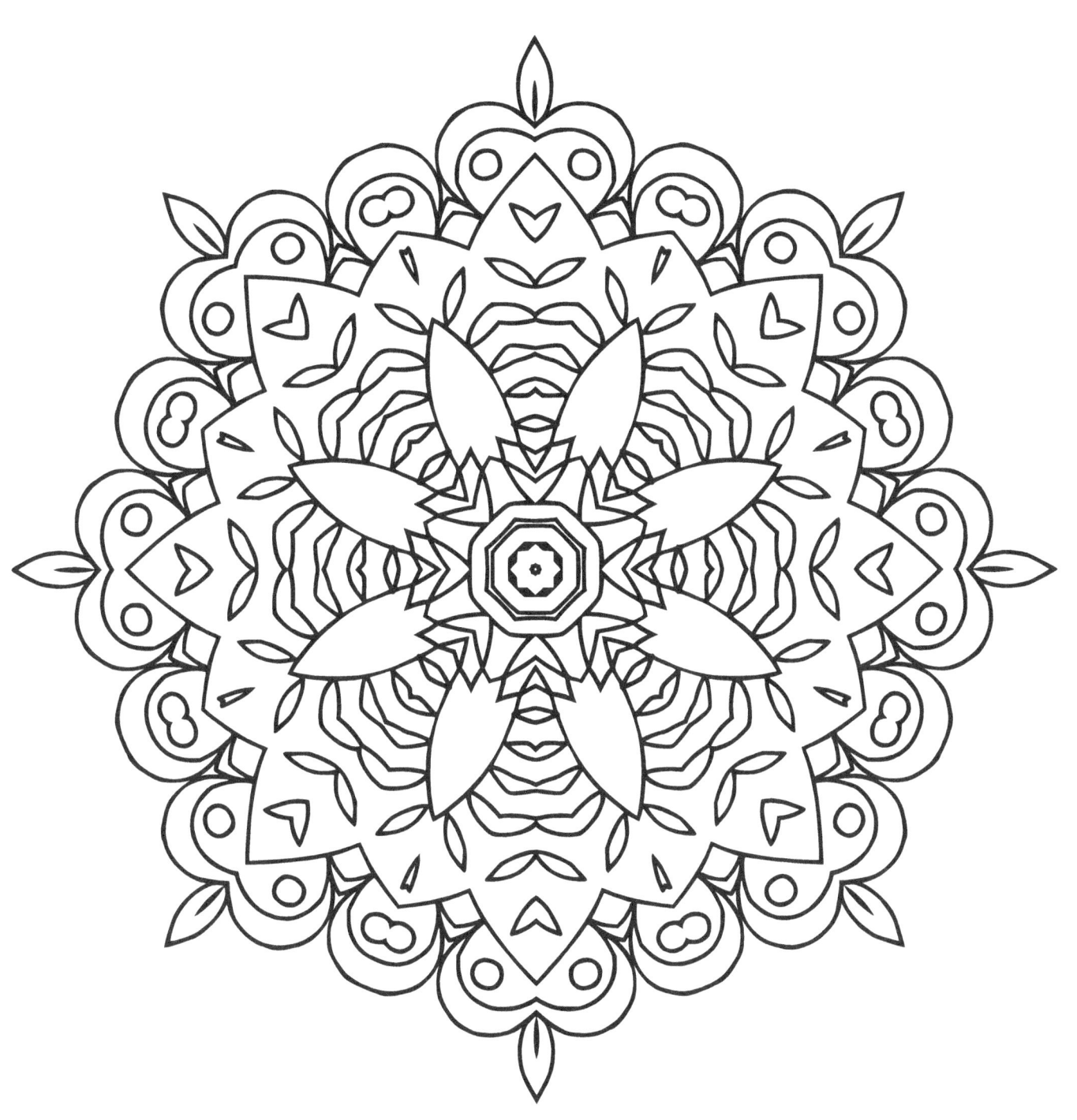

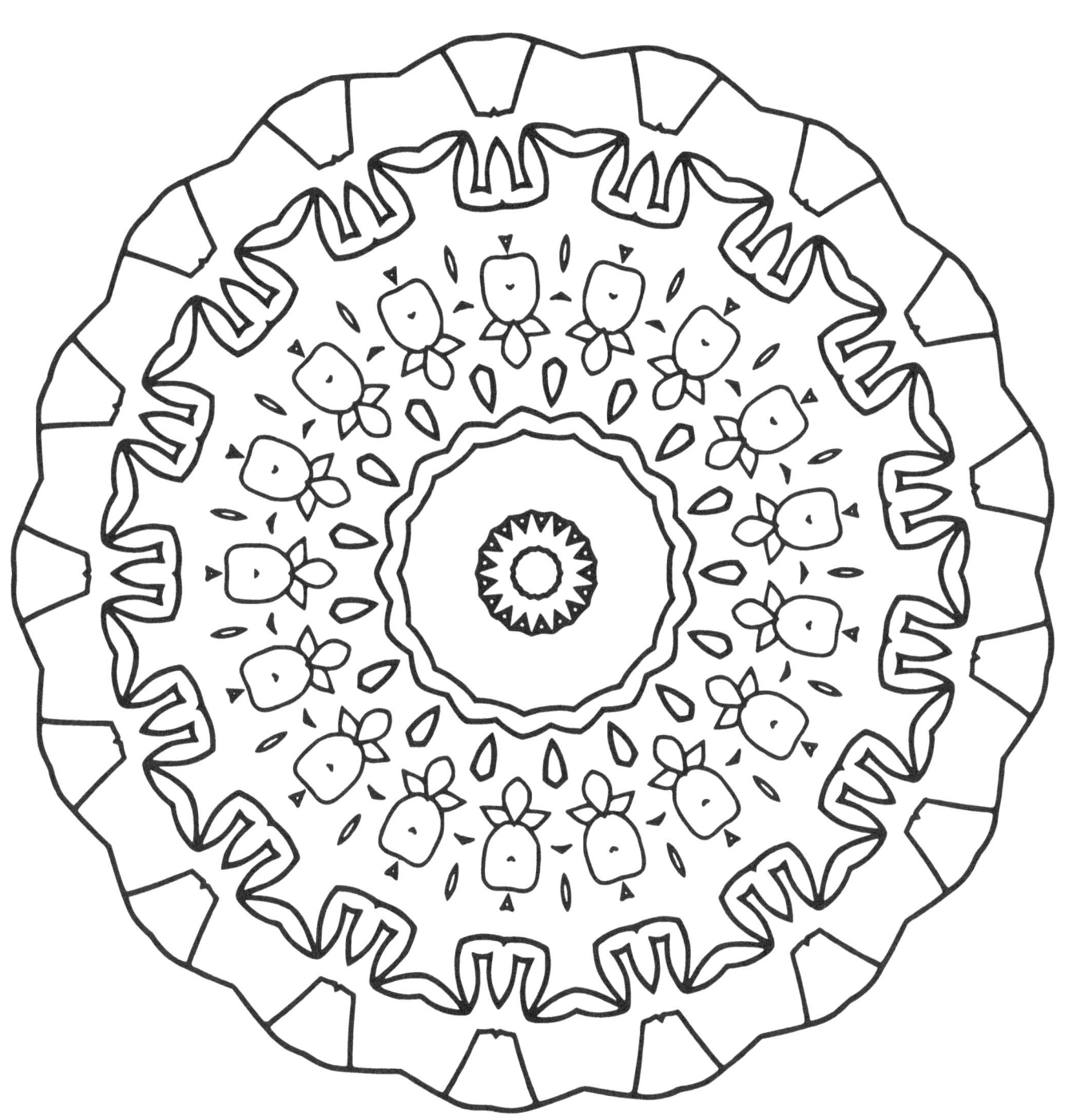

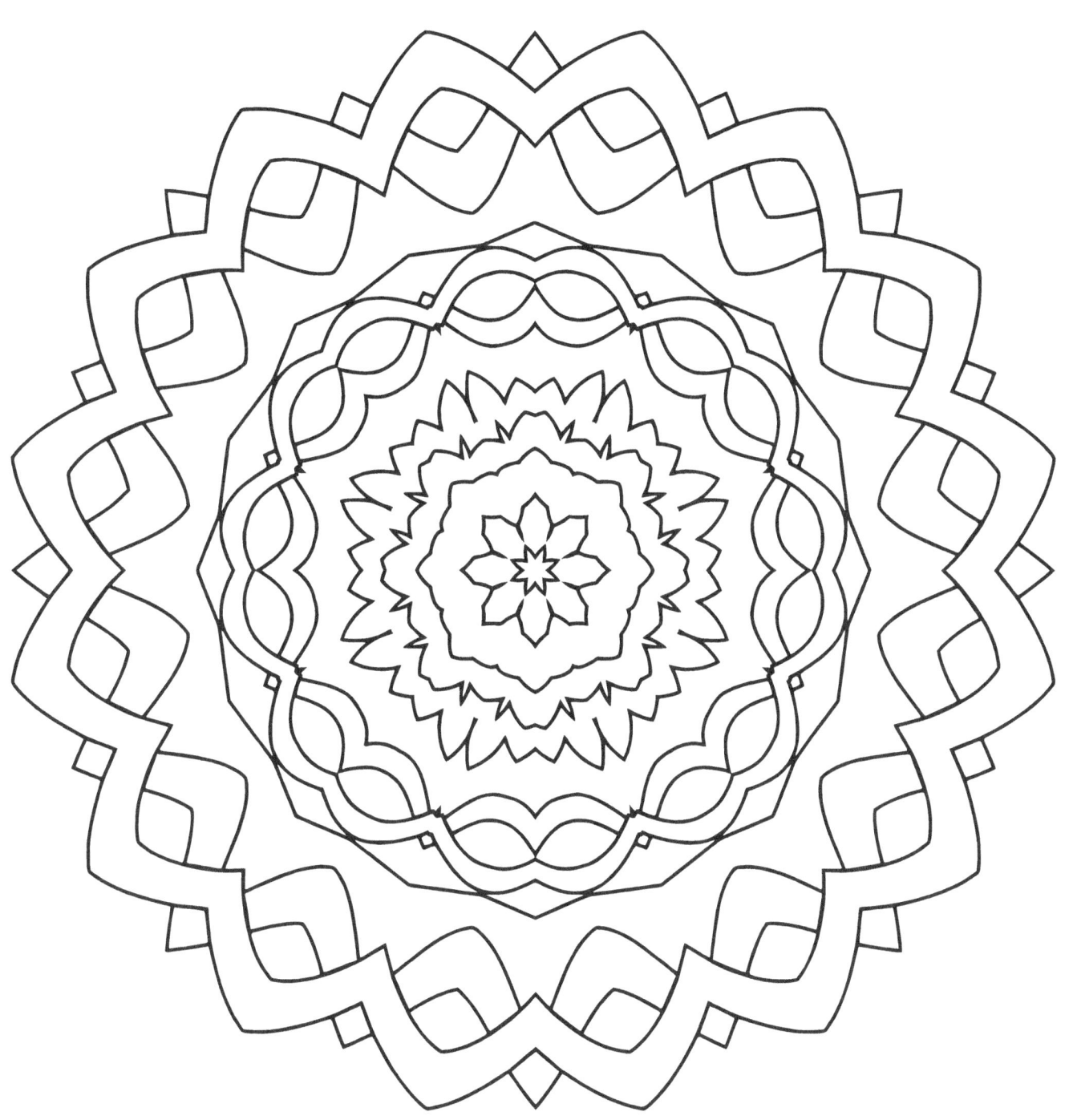

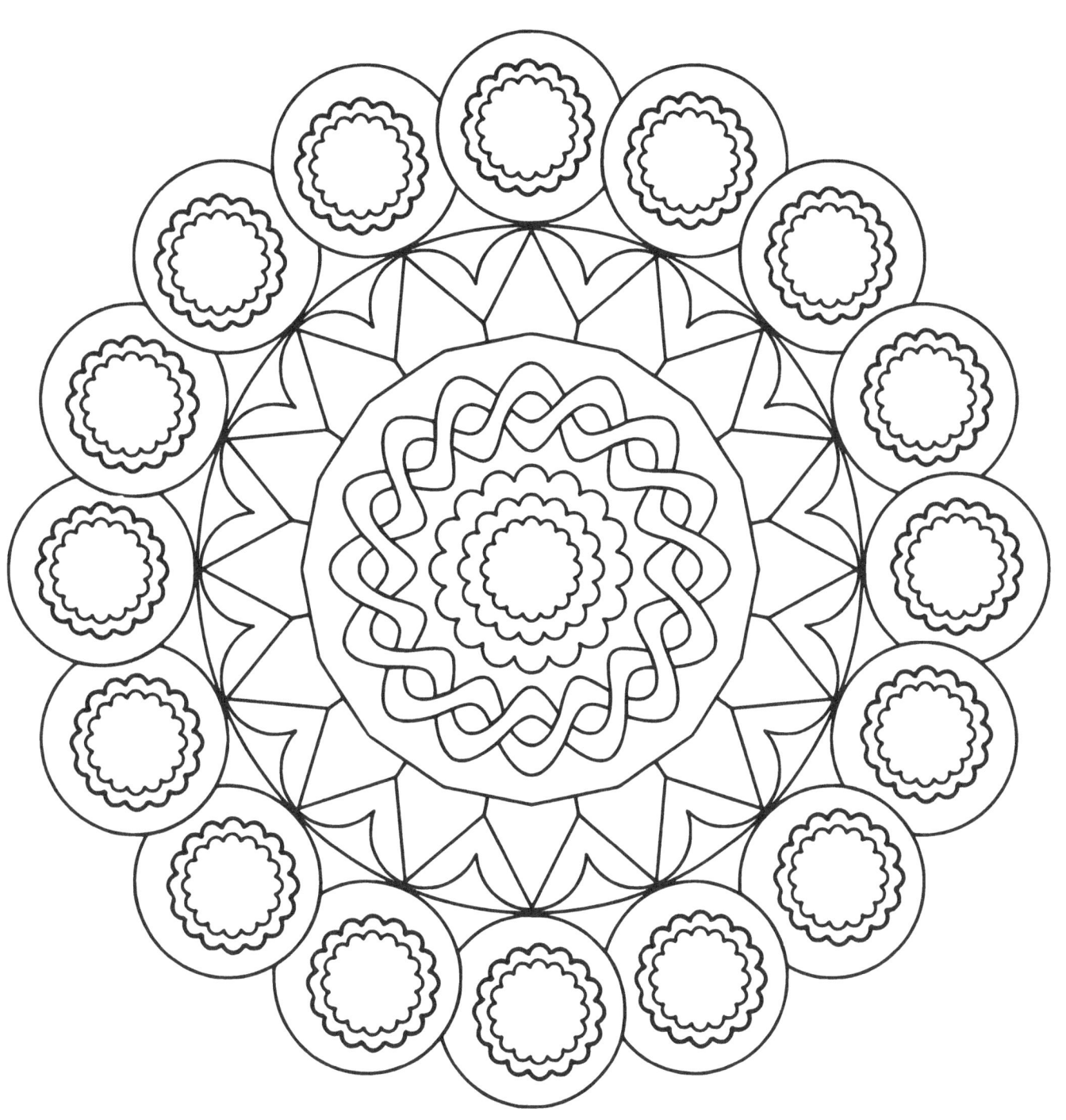

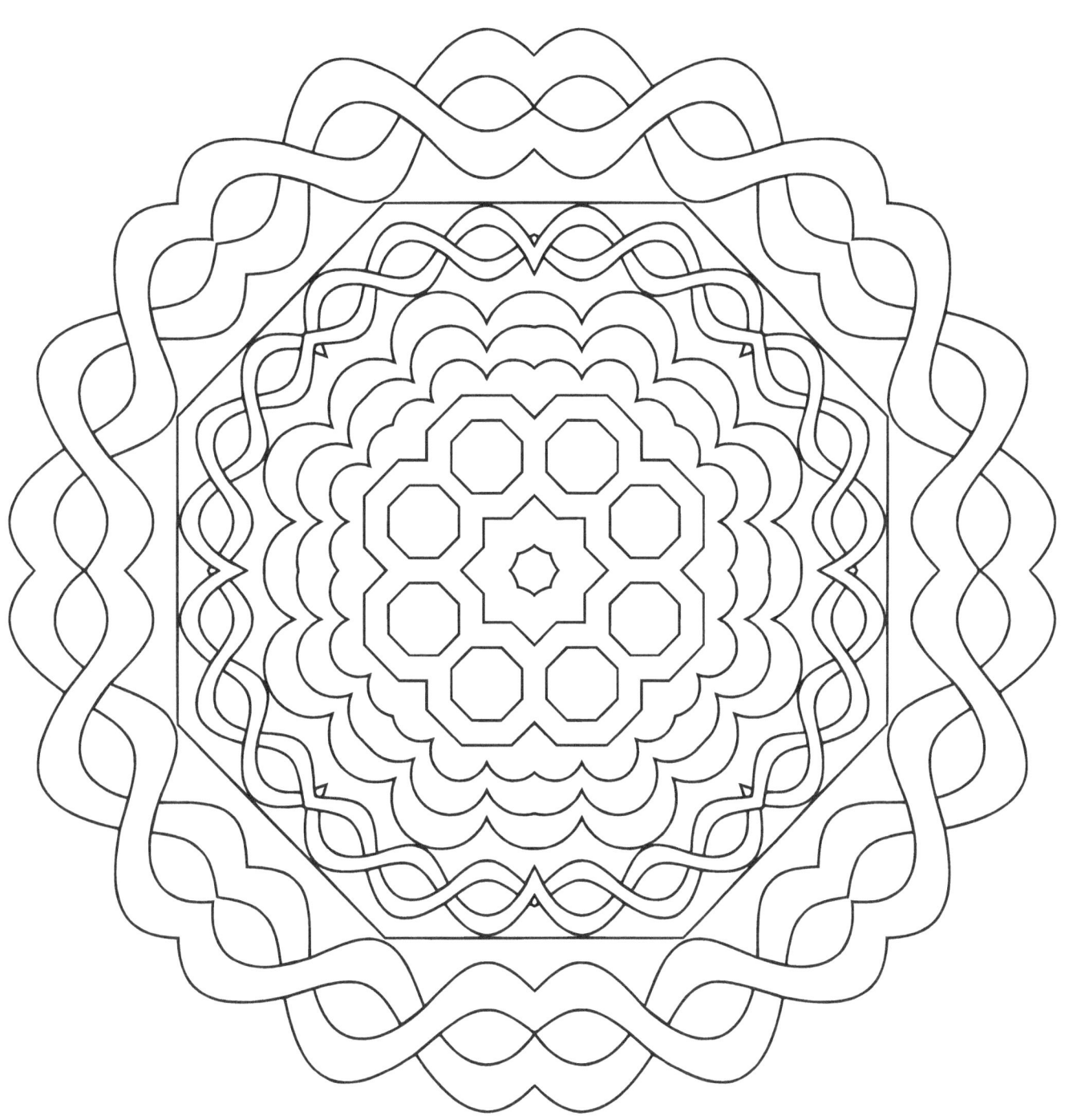

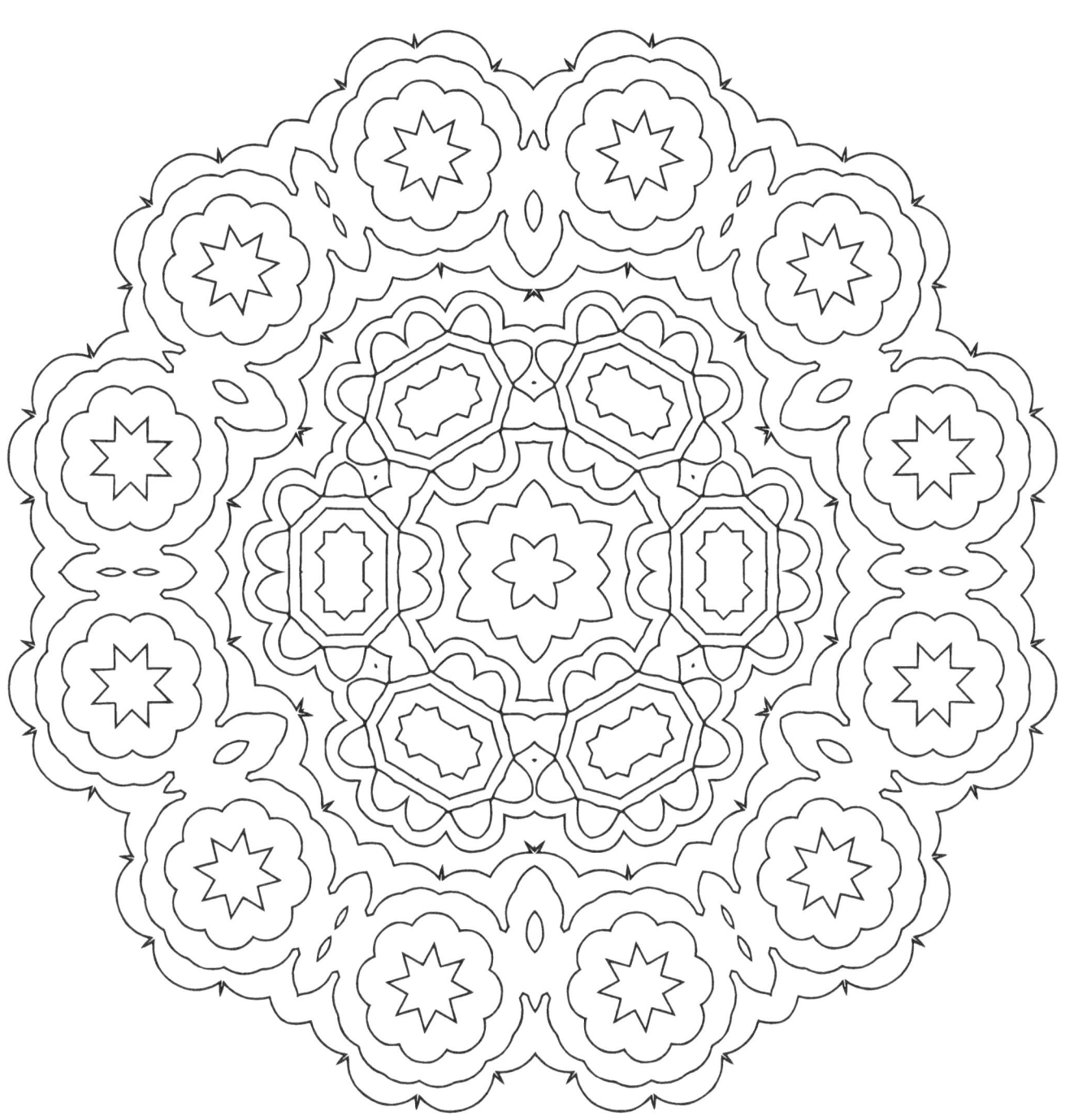

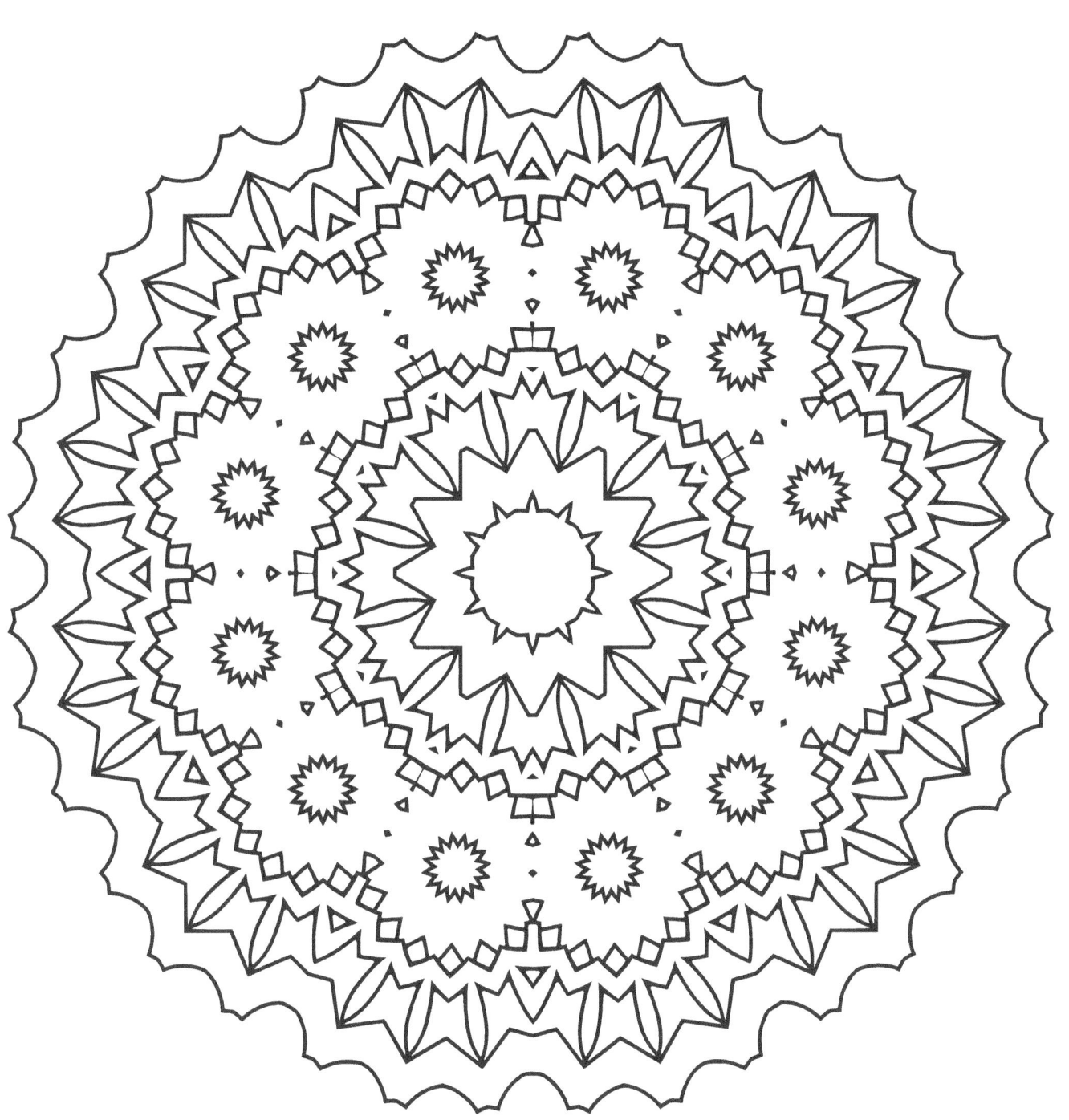

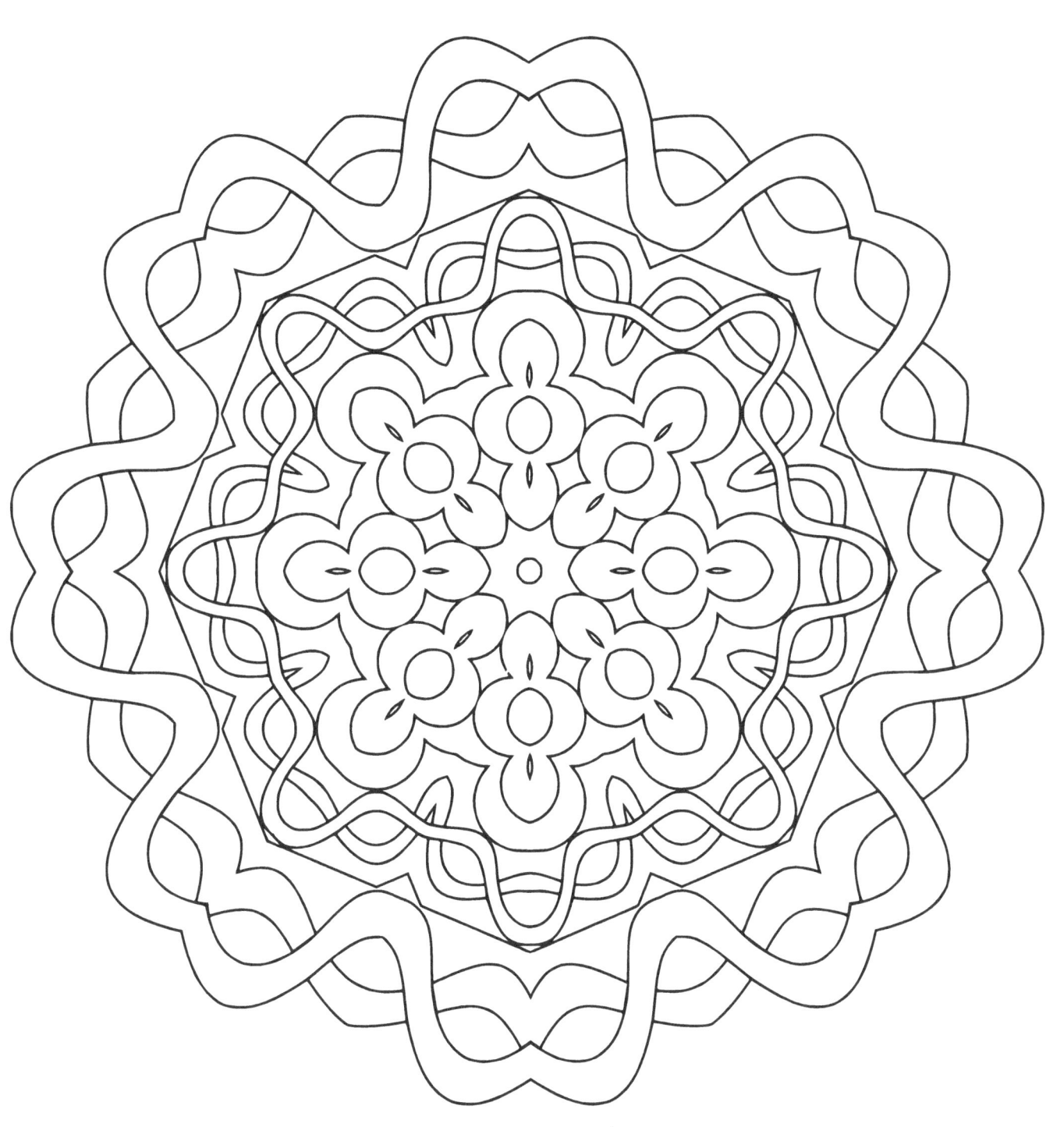

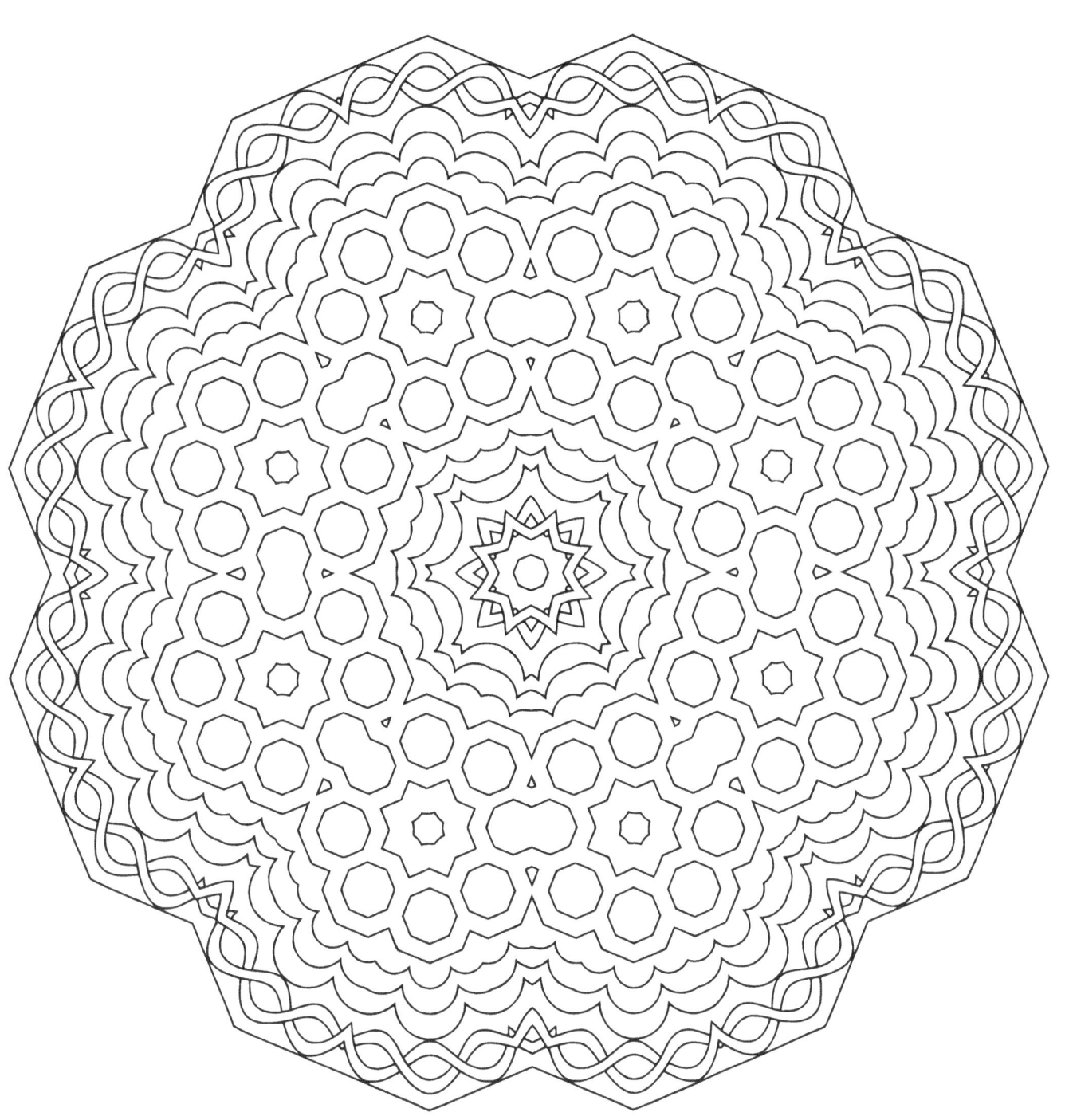

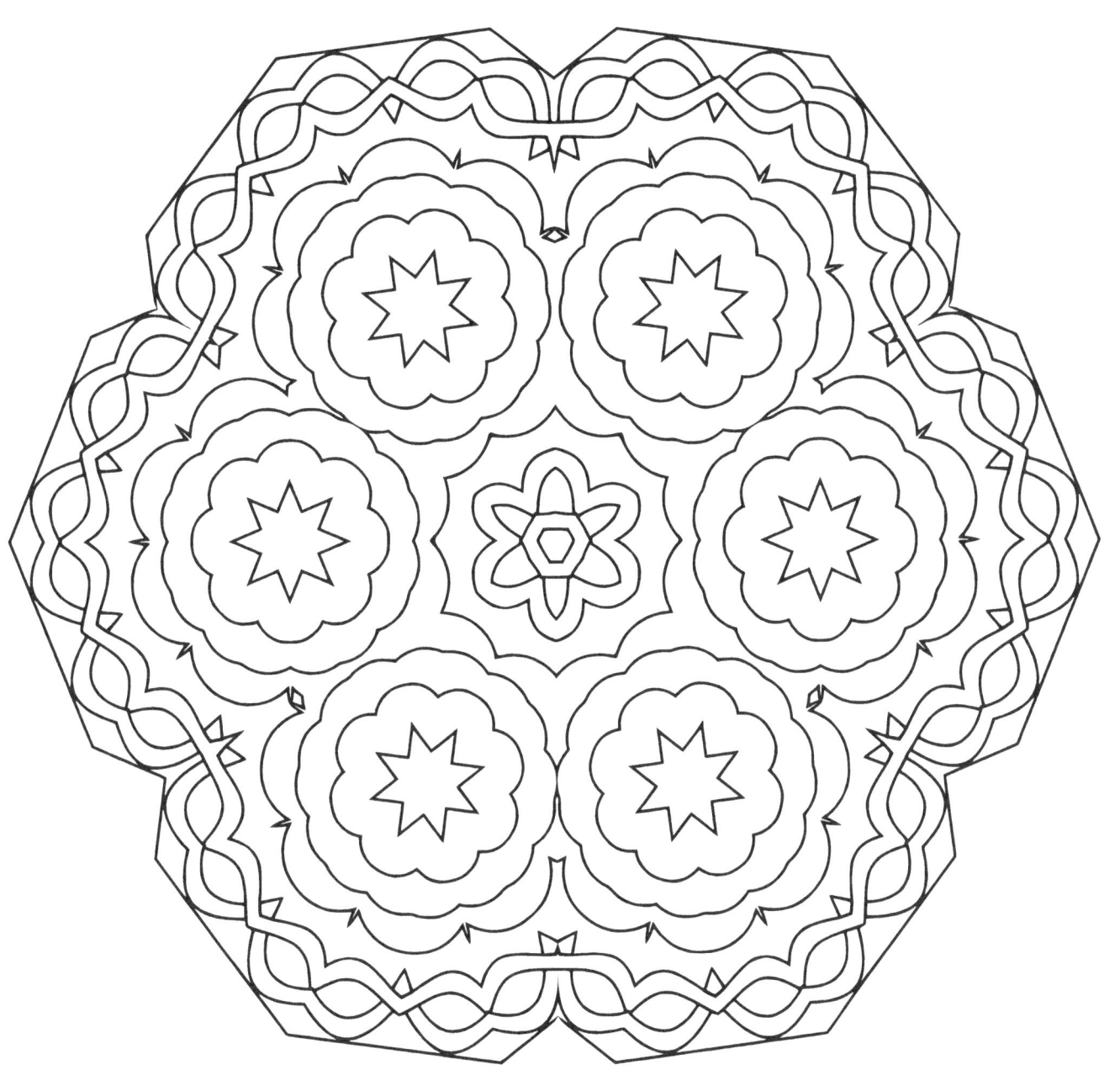

Thank You and Some Free Samples

At the moment I have two additional Easy Mandala books available so i am including samples from those books here so you can have an idea what they are like. On the following pages you will find samples from Easy Mandalas 2 and Easy Mandalas 3. I will provide links to these books on Amazon as well. Hope you enjoy these free pages and that you will explore these other books.

And I want to thank you for purchasing my coloring book. I hope you have had many happy hours coloring the pictures in it. I am currently working on additional coloring books that you might enjoy.

If you'd like me to notify you when I have new books coming out or if you'd like to receive free pages occasionally, you can do so by joining my newsletter. Just go to www.coloringfunforadults.com/subscribe to join.

And please come visit my website and get some free coloring pages as well as coloring tips and more. To access my website, just go to www.coloringfunforadults.com

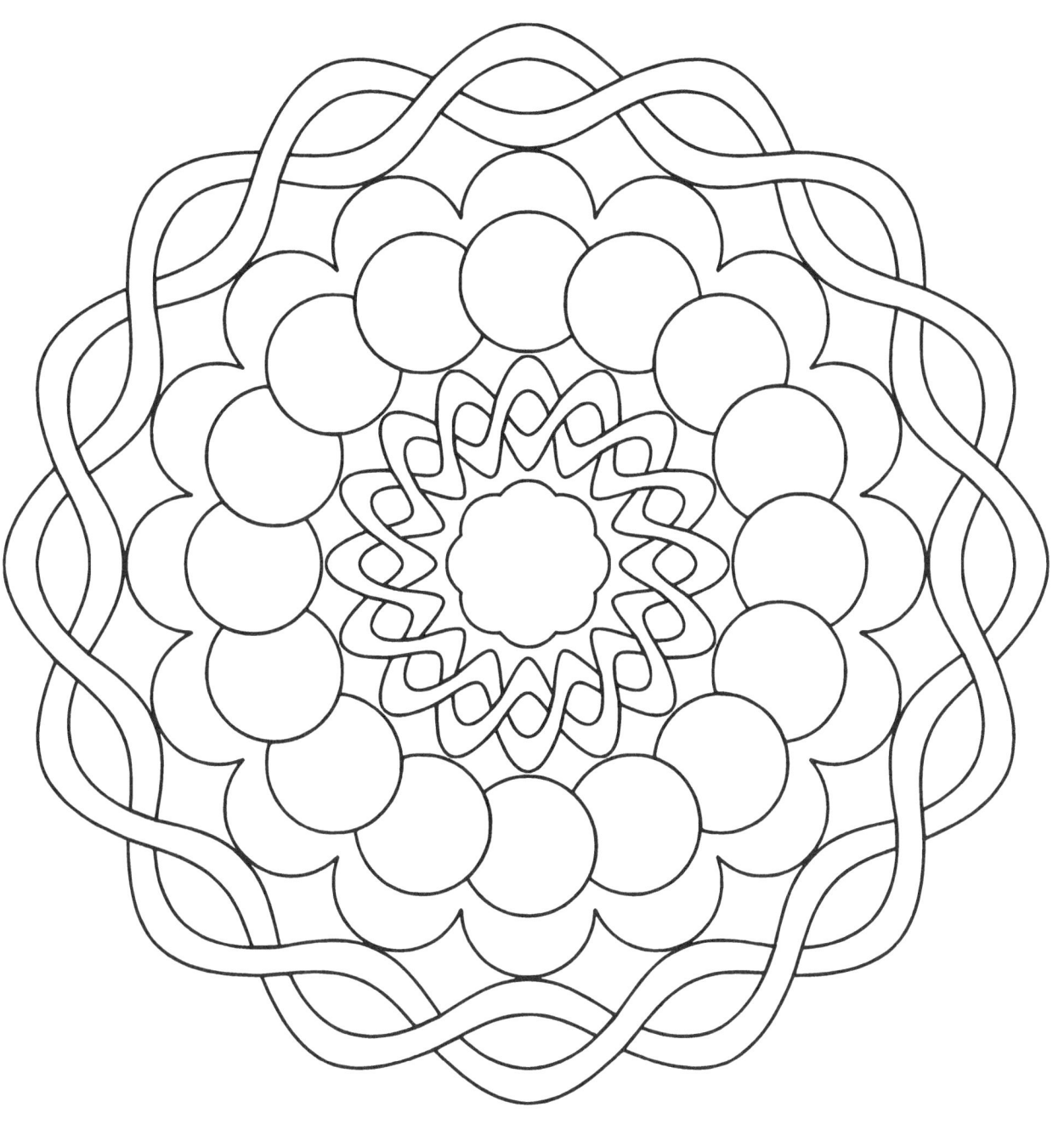

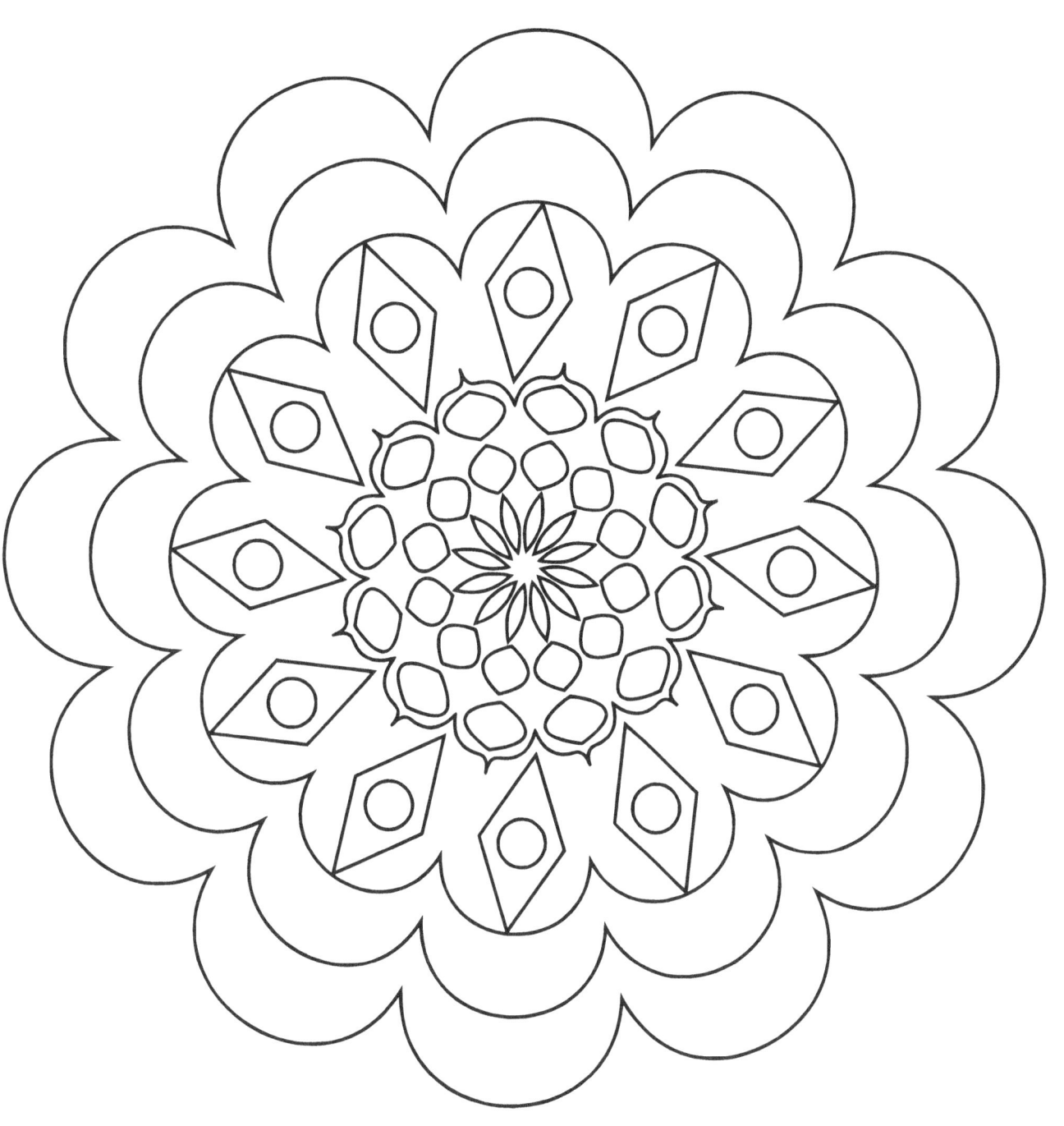